The Craftsman's Art Series

# The Craft of
# Weaving

Irene Waller

Stanley Paul, London

Stanley Paul & Co Ltd
3 Fitzroy Square, London W1P 6JD

An imprint of the Hutchinson Publishing Group Ltd

London Melbourne Sydney Auckland
Wellington Johannesburg and agencies
throughout the world

First published 1976
© Irene Waller 1976
Drawings © Irene Waller 1976

Printed in Great Britain by litho by The Anchor Press Ltd
and bound by Wm Brendon & Son Ltd
both of Tiptree, Essex

ISBN 0 09 125320 9 (cased)
      0 09 125321 7 (paper)

*Contents*

,

reed and heddles together – The use of the rigid heddle to speed weaving and control the width

# Acknowledgements

Photographs were taken by the following photographers:

Martin Westley: 3, 5, 6, 7, 8, 11, 12, 13, 14, 15, 16, 17, 18, 22, 23, 24, 24a, 25, 26, 27, 28, 29, 30, 31, 32, 33, 34, 35, 36, 37, 38, 47, 48, 49, 54.
Alan Hill: 2, 41, 58, 61, 62, 63.
Ferdinand Boesch: 39.
Dr Robert Burningham: 65.
Irene Waller: 20, 40, 42, 43, 52a, 53, 56, 57, 60, 64, 66, 67, 68, 69, 70, 71, 72.

Drawings by the Author.
All work not otherwise credited, by the Author.

# 1 Introduction

The aim of this book is to take the non-weaver, someone who knows nothing about the subject, slowly, stage by stage, through various technically simple projects, producing a specific object each time. Nothing is left to chance or conjecture, everything explained. Materials used are those easily and quickly available and where it is possible to have the satisfaction of re-cycling already used materials this is suggested. Equipment used is of the very simplest and wherever possible it is constructed from elements near at hand.

The book is intended to be worked through, page by page, rather as if you were working with a teacher in a class. This way you can learn by practical experience, slowly building up a sound basic knowledge of the process of weaving and laying a firm foundation for later work.

All the objects suggested as projects were woven especially for the book while it was being written, to make as sure as possible that the instructions and the objects really work.

Weaving has its own distinct vocabulary. Some of its words may be totally unfamiliar, others have a different meaning in everyday use. To help you here there is a glossary on page 87. Turn to this if you are in any doubt.

## What Weaving Is

Weaving is the interlacing together of two distinct and separate sets or 'sheets' of threads (unlike knitting or crochet, both of which are the constant interlooping of one continuous thread). The two sets of threads lie at right angles to each other. One set (think of this as vertical for the moment) is called the *warp*, and the other set, the horizontal, is called the *weft*. The two interlaced together form the structure (fig 1).

ontispiece *(Above)* 'Situation Quadrangulaire 1975' Daniel Graffin, Paris.
vast three-dimensional textile object constructed in plain weave.
*Below)* Detail of weave.

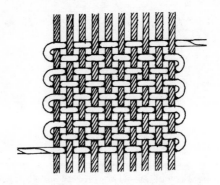

1. The plain weave construction.

## How Weaving is Done

The warp threads are your first consideration as these are the threads which are placed onto the loom (dark, in the diagram). A loom is only a frame on which the warp threads are held – that and nothing more. Looms can be very intimidating to look at. Some of them are complex with a lot of incomprehensible strings, hooks and loops and people who can use looms are sometimes regarded as rather accomplished. But all this is nonsense. A loom is a frame to hold the warp threads taut and under control so that they are ready to have the second set of threads, the weft, passed through them.

The weft thread is, one long, continuous thread, which passes across and through the warp threads from right to left, then from left to right and so on, thus gradually building up the woven structure recognizable as cloth (light, in the diagram).

Two things are necessary for weaving to take place: (1) each warp thread (or warp 'end') must be capable of being individually lifted or left down in order to allow the weft to pass through; (2) the weft thread must be wound onto something, a needle, shuttle-stick, or even just wound into a small skein, in order to ease its passage through the warp ends.

The simplest weave construction is the 'one under and one over' sequence seen in fig 1 called 'plain' or 'tabby' weaving. As the weft passes from right to left, it passes over the first warp end, under the second, over the third, under the fourth, and so on. On its passage back, from left to right, it passes under where it previously passed over, and over where it previously passed under. You may be familiar with this in the form of darning and sacking. It is also the basis of much of the woven cloth we wear and use in the home. This is not always immediately recognizable because much cloth is fine and therefore the weave structure is not easy to see.

A magnifying glass will show you in detail how the cloth in your home is made. With the glass, take a good close look at your cushions, upholstery, curtains, sweaters, coats and dresses. You may well find, under magnification, that a fair percentage of the fabric of which these things are made is knitted because this is a very economical method of producing textiles in bulk. But you will find that your tea-towels, pillows, sheets and some tablecloths are mostly formed by the tabby weave, and possibly much of your clothing too. You may see something which is obviously woven, i.e. it has two sheets of threads interlacing with each other at right angles, but yet it is not recognizable as a tabby weave. Even then much of what has been discussed still applies. It is merely that the weft thread has passed through the warp threads in some other sequence than 'one over, one under'.

One very satisfactory thing about weaving is that the basic, plain weave holds a thousand possibilities for invention and design. One could weave the plain construction all one's life and still not run out of possibilities (see frontispiece and fig 45). The reason is that weaving is made up of two elements, the construction and the actual yarns. The yarns, in turn, can be made in many different ways (fig 2), in many fibres and in many different colours. So, the type of fibre, the design of the yarn and the colour of the yarn or yarns are all quite simple factors which can give immediate design variation. To illustrate this, compare household string with knitting wool. Look at them under the magnifying glass and feel them. They are both yarn but very different in their feel, look and behaviour.

Weaving is both visual and tactile. You must use your eyes in the true sense, to look at and analyse how cloth is made, and you must also learn to feel things as well as to look at them. With your eyes closed, feel the difference between the skirt and the sweater you may be wearing, or the upholstery of your chair compared to the carpet on the floor. Carpets and some upholstery fabric and towels are hard to analyse as you may only be aware of a mass of yarn ends which are the cut surface of the pile, but a pile, i.e. tufts of thread, can be inserted into a knitted or a woven construction.

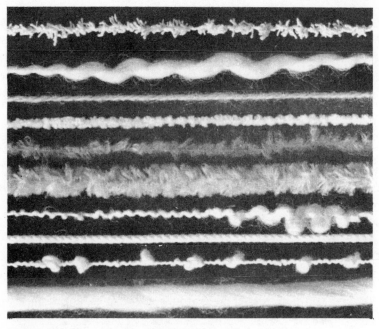

**2.** Weaving yarns constructed in various ways.
Cotton snarl, wool cloud yarn, two-ply wool, chenille, textured Taslan,
*'Furwul'*, gimp made of slub yarn, two-ply cotton, cotton knop, wool roving.

When a woven construction has a pile then the pile makes a third set of threads: warps (vertical), weft (horizontal) and pile (three-dimensional).

It seems to me that there are two main reasons why you might want to weave. One is the desire to make an object of practical use with your own hands and to your own design specifications. For instance, you may have acquired a white dining table and want brown place-mats for it. You may need cushions of a particular range of ochres to place upon a particular sofa. In these instances it is maddening not to be able to get what you want, so to produce it yourself gives a double satisfaction.

The second reason is more abstract. Weaving is the method of textile construction which out of all the others (lace, crochet, knitting) gives us the greatest scope for the imaginative use of fibre, yarns and a great many other materials also, like polythene, ribbons, beads or fur. The weave construction can be the total picture (fig 1) or it can be subdued to produce a weft-dominated surface of heavy pile (fig 38) or encrustations of rich materials (fig 55) or, as in tapestry, to form free graphic images (fig 39).

So, weaving is not limited, but the very reverse, a technique which has great technical and artistic possibilities. It is something which can be pursued fairly easily at home. There is a method and a piece of equipment to suit all needs. whether you want to weave on your lap, or whether you have a spare room and want to invest in floor and table looms.

But, most of all, the materials and constructions used in weaving satisfy the mind, the eye and the fingertips.

### The Special Satisfactions of Weaving

'You don't know whether you like it until you try it' is fair comment. Beginners do not necessarily know whether they will get 'hooked' or whether weaving will leave them cold. This is an excellent reason for following the procedure outlined in this book, which is to start from the very simple basic concepts and methods. If you do this you will not have frightened yourself with complex ideas and equipment, or incurred great expense.

The hand-knitter knows the satisfaction of feeling fine, smooth wool in her hands, or the visual and tactile pleasure of evenly knitted fabric structure, the satisfactory weight of knitted fabric hanging from the needles and falling over her hands. The equivalent of these practical pleasures, for the weaver, is the satisfaction of setting the warp threads on the loom in a 'sheet' of evenly tensioned parallel threads – like a musical instrument. The next pleasure is viewing the completed warp, like a painter his newly sized canvas, and speculating upon the coming splendour of the resulting weave when the chosen weft has been inserted. The action of opening the warp threads to allow the weft through is both a visual and a tactile pleasure, so is inserting the weft and pressing down the weft threads, 'pick' (row) by pick, so that the warp is gradually overcome by the encroaching weft, advancing in an impeccable horizontal line. The final woven structure should be the most satisfactory part of all if the fibres, yarns, colours and the manner in which they are used have been well chosen, not to mention the triumphal moment of removing the piece of work from the loom when it relaxes and takes on the pliant, supple characteristics of a textile object.

Weaving can be to a practical end, like cloth yardage and textile objects: mats, cushions, clothes. But it can also be used as a totally abstract fine art form. The weaver can use the warp and loom as a means and catalyst for his or her creative thought processes. This has progressed in the art world to such a degree that we have come to a moment in time when the sculptors and some of the great textile artists are speaking the same language, even though they have reached their goal by different routes (see frontispiece and fig 45).

For most of us, our aim is something between the two. It is good to make a personal and aesthetically satisfying statement in even the most utilitarian of practical projects. After all, apart from the purely practical satisfaction of working with the hands, there is little intelligence needed or satisfaction gained in reproducing a machine-made object or reproducing something already in existence.

At the other end of the scale it is not given to all of us to make great artistic statements or even to be able to give satisfactory substance to our abstract concepts, but we can give freedom to our imaginations via the loom, without feeling too inhibited, as the materials with which we work are familiar domestic ones.

# 2 Simple Beginnings: The Weaving Frame

It is quite possible to begin the process of weaving without any equipment at all. One can, for example, bend a flexible tree branch or piece of strong wire into a U-form and stretch the foundation threads, the warp, between the two arms of the U. But somewhere between this primitive makeshift and the purchase of specialist equipment, there is the middle way, which enables the weaver to make an artefact of a reasonable size, with fair speed and competence, with a minimum of previous know-how and little expense. This middle way is the construction and use of a wooden frame and it is made as follows:

## How to Make the Weaving Frame

Materials needed:

Two pieces of wood 710mm × 38mm × 12mm (28in × 1½in × ½in).

Two pieces of wood 450mm × 38mm × 25mm (18in × 1½in × 1in).

These four pieces should be of planed deal or other softwood as this is easy to work and cheap. They are to make the four sides of the frame.

One piece of wood 508mm × 25mm × 4·5mm (20in × 1in × $\frac{3}{16}$in).

Two pieces of wood 450mm × 50mm × 4·5mm (18in × 2in × $\frac{3}{16}$in).

These last three pieces should be of white, birch plywood, which is very smooth and fine-grained. They are to make a shed-stick which holds the threads apart to allow the shed-stick through and also the shuttle-sticks, which hold the yarn with which one weaves (see page 15).

Woodworker's adhesive (quick-setting epoxy resin is excellent).

A large ball or balls of average weight, smooth, white household string 45m (50 yards).

Sixteen 50mm (2in) panel pins, about seventy 25mm (1in) panel pins.

Some sandpaper for smoothing.

A hammer and a small saw.

*Assembling the frame*

On a flat table-top and with the aid of a set-square to ensure square corners, place the two 710mm (28in) pieces of deal on their 12mm ($\frac{1}{2}$in) sides 430mm (17in) apart. Now place the two 450mm (18in) pieces of deal on their 25mm (1in) sides at either end and butting over the 710mm (28in) pieces. Apply woodworker's adhesive to the ends of the 710mm (28in) pieces, fit the frame together and allow it to dry for the necessary length of time under pressure. Then secure the corners with the panel-pins. More complex corners are permissible to the ardent woodworker. Smooth the frame with sandpaper. Next, make a pencil line along the middle of the 25mm (1in) edge of the 450mm (18in) ends and mark off at 12mm ($\frac{1}{2}$in) intervals. At one end the 12mm ($\frac{1}{2}$in) marks should begin 12mm ($\frac{1}{2}$in) in from the inner edge of the frame and at the other end 6mm ($\frac{1}{4}$in) in from the inner edge of the frame. Now drive a 25mm (1in) panel-pin into each mark, leaving 12mm ($\frac{1}{2}$in) protruding. These are the projections on which you will wind your foundation threads, the warp. If the wood shows any inclination to split, then stagger the panel-pins slightly, but they are much better in a straight line.

The length of birch ply 508mm (20in) long needs only a smoothing with sandpaper.

The final procedure is to make the two shuttle-sticks which are the yarn carriers. At each end of both sticks, with a pencil, make a line 50mm (2in) from the end. Then, between this line and the ends, make two lines 12mm ($\frac{1}{2}$in) in from the side edges. Now draw two half-circle curves at the end of each stick on the two 12mm ($\frac{1}{2}$in) spaces, and a larger half-circle curve in the opposite direction on the 25mm (1in) space. Use the saw to cut around the resulting shape and smooth this off very carefully.

You are now ready to prepare this simple loom with the initial threads ready for weaving (fig 3).

*Alternatives to the made frame*

If the purchase of wood is difficult, or the would-be weaver totally ham-fisted with a hammer and nails, and there is no talented friend to rise to the challenge, then there are several alternative possibilities. Find a picture frame or deck-chair frame. It must be clean, smooth, sturdy and as large as or larger than the constructed wooden frame.

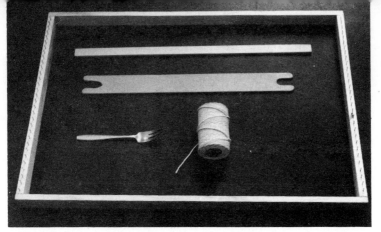

3. The weaving frame, shed-stick and shuttle-stick.

A weaving frame cannot be wobbly or splintery! Now drive in the panel-pins at both the shorter ends – this cannot be avoided and the accuracy of placing and the correct number is important. Use a long ruler instead of the 508mm (20in) piece of birch ply. Make a 'butterfly' of the weft yarn instead of winding it on shuttle-sticks (fig. 4). The 'butterfly' of yarn can be unsatisfactory and annoying. Only use it temporarily. It is much better to buy some shuttle-sticks (see Suppliers).

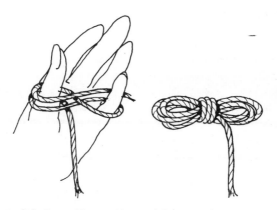

4. The 'butterfly' of yarn. The working end draws out from the middle.

**Setting on the Warp**

Knot the household string firmly around the panel pin which is placed 6mm (¼in) from the inner edge of the frame. Take it to the other end of the frame and around the first pin there (12mm (½in) from inner edge). Wind the string back and forth until the frame is entirely wound and knot off firmly. The tension of the wound string should be 'comfortable', neither sloppy nor too tight. If it is too sloppy, it will come off the panel pins. If it is too tight, you will not be able to separate the warp threads when you come to insert the weft. Once you have set on these threads you have 'wound the warp', a technical textile term which indicates the threads which run the length of any cloth. These are always the stronger of the two sets of threads which compose the woven structure because they must withstand a great deal of wear and tension. The warp must always be most carefully chosen. In any weaving it is a fair test to subject one's proposed warp thread to considerable rubbing and friction to see if it will stand up to the stresses of its function.

**Preparation for Weaving**

Take the 508mm (20in) stick in the right hand and thread it over and under the separate threads all the way across the warp. It is now ready for use. You will see that when turned on end it separates the warp threads, every even one up and every odd one down, or vice versa. The stick is called the 'shed stick' and the opening in the threads is the 'shed'.

5. The warped frame with shed-stick inserted and shuttle wound.

You are now absolutely ready to weave (fig 5). The string warp will serve as a suitable basis for many objects and is the ground for the mats, bags and rugs in chapters 3, 4, 5 and 6. No more can be done until you have considered your object. The weft is the thread which travels across the fabric, from selvedge to selvedge. Because it goes through the open shed it can be of almost any thickness or texture and has no such constraints as has the warp. You will now understand why, when making woven fabric into garments or furnishings, it is so important to have the warp or longitudinal threads hanging vertically and the weft horizontally. Obviously, if the stronger threads run vertically down your dress or your curtains, these will fold and hang well.

# 3 Simple Weaving on the Frame, Three Mats

In any woven structure, having set the warp on the weaving frame, the next consideration is the fibre content, texture, weight and colour of the weft yarn. Obviously one must consider the effect of the warp and weft when interlaced together, as it is this procedure which produces the final visual effect. This is normally done at the very outset of a project. In this case I have suggested setting on a string warp. It will behave well as a new weaver's first warp, it is easy to obtain and it provides a satisfactory basis for several different projects. Therefore, in this instance, certain materials are suggested equally arbitrarily for the weft as there is every chance that they will work and there is nothing like a little initial success to spur one on.

## The Place Mats

You now need a weft yarn for the place mats. There are two main possibilities, (1) thick natural coloured jute garden twine or, if you live in the country baler twine and (2) natural or coloured garden raffia. So, take a trip to the garden shop and take on supplies. The jute garden twine should be the thickest, softest and fullest you can get; if it is too hard, fine and tightly spun, then don't use it, go for raffia instead.

Wind some jute, either singly or double (if double from two balls at once), on to the shuttle-stick. Wind a few turns around the width of the stick at one end to secure the yarn firmly and then wind along the length of the stick (fig 5). Do not, at first, ever wind too much weft yarn on a shuttle-stick as this can make it difficult to get the stick and yarn through the 25mm (1in) deep shed. Also, you may change your mind about your choice of weft yarn and thus have wasted time and yarn. If you are using raffia, which will be in lengths, put one piece around the shuttle-stick.

Now settle yourself in a comfortable weaving position. I find that

I like to sit either at a table or in front of a wall or window so that I can wedge the frame very firmly between me and something stable. The frame must be steady and under control and must not joggle about. The frame loom can have a channel cut in the far narrow end of the frame so that it fits snugly onto the table edge. Clever carpenters take note.

Make sure you have all you need on a small table by your right hand, so that once wedged you do not have to get up again. You need the wound shuttle, more yarn, sharp scissors, a very strong, coarse household fork (the shorter and fewer the prongs the better) (fig 3) and a piece of stiff brown paper or card 50mm × 508mm (2in × 20in).

First thread the piece of stiff paper through the warp threads, under two, over two, right across and push it down firmly to the bottom of the warp: this will give you a space for a fringe at the edge of the mat.

Next, turn the shed-stick, which has already been threaded through the warp (page 16) on end. Through the resulting opening (the 'shed') pass the shuttle-stick from left to right (if you are left-handed, the reverse) with about a metre (or approximately a yard) of yarn trailing. Pull the yarn through until 38mm (1½in) of yarn is still protruding on the left side of the warp. With your fingers, take this around the end warp thread and back through the shed so that the weft doubles back on itself. This is the method of starting the weft neatly which will be suggested throughout the book (fig 6). With the fork, press the yarn down firmly to the brown paper, begin from the left and work to the right allowing the jute weft to ride comfortably over and under the taut warp threads.

6. Starting the weft thread.

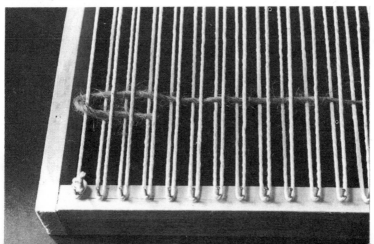

7. Making an arc with the weft.    8. Pressing the weft into place.

With the shed-stick pushed as far back out of the way as possible, now thread the shuttle-stick through the warp threads from right to left in the opposite sequence to the preceding 'pick' (row), i.e. over a warp and where the last weft was under and vice versa. Pull the yarn through, not straight, but at an angle away from you while holding the right-hand warp ends firmly between the right finger and thumb. Then bring the yarn down in an arc (fig 7) and press it firmly in place with the fork. Begin pressing from the centre and work outwards again, making sure that the weft rides comfortably over and under the taut warp threads (fig 8). Remember that you are interlacing the two sets of threads together: the warp is held taut and cannot 'give' and therefore the weft must (fig 9).

9. End-on view of weft passing over and under the warp ends.

You can now continue to weave, using the shed-stick to make the passage for the shuttle-stick and weft when passing from left to right and threading the shuttle-stick through manually when passing from right to left (left-handers reverse the procedure). When performing this operation, place the left hand gently over the warp ends to steady them so that the shuttle-stick can pass over and under them efficiently and swiftly: the shuttle 'pursues' the left hand. If this movement seems clumsy, make sure the end of the shuttle is really smooth and, if not, sand it again.

This, then, is the process of plain or tabby weaving on the simple frame. Plain weaving is as aesthetically satisfying as any other construction providing the yarns and colours chosen are pleasing and the weaving is even and a satisfactory weight and texture.

It is at this point that one must stress yet again a most elementary but important factor in the production of even weaving. *Every individual warp end must remain in an absolutely parallel line to the next, and every weft pick must also take an absolutely parallel line to the next one and lie at an exact right angle to the warp* (look again at fig 1). You may have little difficulty in keeping the warp ends at right angles to the weft because they are held taut on the panel pins. But, as weaving progresses, you might have difficulty in keeping them exactly parallel *to each other* because on this frame there is no mechanism (on other looms called a reed or spacer) to keep each one in its exact, correct longitudinal position. Moreover, the action of pulling the weft through the warp from right to left and left to right tends to make the whole piece of weaving develop a 'waist' and also to bunch the warp ends together in the middle, leaving the sides sparse. You should avoid this at all cost.

To overcome it is technically simple but requires visual, and tactile sensitivity. It is a matter of appreciating that the warp ends are held comparatively taut and cannot 'give'. The weft takes an 'over and under' path and, what is more, the opposite path on every pick. Therefore, if the warps cannot give then the weft must: there must be more weft yarn available for the 'over and under' corrugated path it is destined to take than would at first seem necessary. Pass the weft yarn on the shuttle-stick through the shed, holding it at an angle until it is bending snugly around the end warp thread, neither too tight nor leaving an ugly loop. Your finger and thumb should be holding the edge against which you are gently pulling. Bring down the weft yarn to the other edge so that it is lying in a large curve or arc within the shed (fig 7). Then press it into place with the fork, starting from the centre or the closed end and working outwards (fig 8). Thus there is enough length of weft yarn to allow it to lie over and under the warp ends, leaving them undisturbed (fig 9). The warp can take on its corrugations when the article is finally released from the loom.

After producing 25mm (1in) or so of cloth, look at it critically and make sure that you can weave correctly, that is produce a fabric in which all warp ends and all weft picks lie absolutely at right angles to each other in every part of the fabric.

Continue to weave in this manner to within 50mm (2in) of the far pins, ending on the left. Take a length of weft yarn from the shuttle-stick, cut it and thread it into a large-eyed needle and hem-stitch across the weaving as in fig 10.

10. Hemstitching. This can be done around one, two, three or four threads.

Hem-stitch the other end, remove the mat from the frame, take out the piece of brown paper and trim the two fringes with sharp scissors. This mat will withstand a great deal of wear and heat and the colour and texture of the soft, thick, natural jute against the smooth, white string should be pleasing and adaptable to almost any setting (fig 11 and fig 14). If you use raffia instead of jute yarn, the main difference in the technique of the weaving is that the raffia is not continuous, in which case, when one piece comes to an end, join the next on by 20mm (¾in) neat overlapping and tuck any recalcitrant ends to the back (fig 12 and 14).

11. Jute place-mat. Close-up of weave.

12. Raffia place-mat. Close-up of weave.

## A Display Mat

To make the display mat, first collect some polythene. Obviously the newer and shinier it is the better and it is very satisfactory to buy new polythene from the stores by the yard. However, it is fair to assume that around the home there will be plenty of clear polythene which has been used as wrapping. The polythene which the dry-cleaners use to cover clothes is fine. My local baker puts the bread in gold polythene bags!

When you think you have enough of the same sort of polythene to start to make a mat, cut it into strips 25mm (1in) wide and 530mm (21in) long. Do not cut too many, experiment first. You may wish to alter the width of the strips. These are individual weft picks and are deliberately crushed when weaving. Weave as before, beginning with the stiff paper. The difference will be that instead of having a continuous weft with neat selvedges at the sides of the work, each weft pick will protrude at either edge about 50mm (2in). When the weaving is finished hem-stitch *all* round the mat. Remove from the loom and trim the string and polythene fringes by placing on the edge of a table, laying a ruler on, and cutting accordingly with sharp scissors. This mat will *not* stand heat and is a display mat only (fig 13 and fig 14); it will look good with pottery and glass and plants (the polythene will withstand damp). You could try one with stripes of white, gold, opaque and black polythene. All three mats are seen in fig 14.

13. Polythene display mat.
Close-up of weave.

14. The jute, raffia and
polythene mats. (See also page 74)

## A Small Bath Mat

If you get a kick from re-cycling materials and have a pile of irri-
tating ancient towels, use them to make a bath mat. But remember
this, old towels will still look like old towels unless you first take
action about the colour. You can give them a certain amount of
new life texturally simply by weaving them anew, but yellowish or
faded towels will still look the same colour, so if you want a white
bath mat and have white towels, bleach them gently to a good white
before starting, otherwise throw the whole lot into a bright dye-bath.
A good scarlet or a clear turquoise or a bright yellow Dylon dye
would transform them into excellent weft material.

Having done this, cut the towelling into 25mm (1in) strips. Sew
these together neatly so that you have long strips which can be
wound on the shuttle-sticks. Weave as for the jute place mat, but
without the paper strips i.e. as far as the nails, crushing the towelling
into place as you did the polythene. Remove the mat from the frame
and weave another. Sew these together by hand along one long side
and edge the resulting 635mm × 860mm (25in × 34in) rectangle with
cotton fringe. Like the polythene display mat, you could produce
another mat in stripes, weaving say 50mm (2in) of black weft and
50mm (2in) of white. Another variation is to weave stripes of terry
towelling weft and stripes of strip sheeting weft, thus producing
textured against smooth areas and using up old sheets in the process.

One final word. The mats are simple in concept and technique and
composed of easily available materials and that is one reason why
they are the first things attempted: but they are *not* all that easy to
weave because you are using a simple frame with no mechanical
assistance whatsoever for creating the woven construction (consider
for a moment the complications of a power loom, which may well
be using all that gadgetry to make just a plain weave). The weft
will 'fight' the warp to a certain extent and you will have to concen-
trate all your attention on preventing the warp ends pulling in,
particularly when weaving with polythene. However, having produced the mats with even reasonable success, you are on your way
to becoming a weaver of skill. The easiest weft yarn to use is rug
wool as this has stretch, softness and resilience but it is obviously
unsuitable for mats. Weaving with rug wool, in order to weave
tapestry, is dealt with in the next chapter.

# 4 Tapestry Bag made on the Frame

## What is Tapestry?

Tapestry is a woven construction of a particular characteristic. It is the plain tabby weave but with one very important difference. The weft is packed down so firmly that in the finished cloth you see only the weft, the warp having been totally obscured. To do this there has to be a special warp-weft relationship, that is the warp must be sparsely spaced and the weft must be put in *very* loosely (see figs 15 and 16). Because only the weft is visible it is possible to produce a textile of unbroken, clear colour, colour areas, and clearly defined patterns and shapes.

The word 'tapestry' is often misused. It is used to describe a certain sort of embroidery, more properly called 'canvas work' and also to describe a cloth indigenous to the Welsh woollen mills, more properly described as double cloth. There are good reasons for both these misnomers. At one point in history true tapestry was imitated by the embroiderers, thus canvas work is miscalled tapestry. The Welsh cloth in question has areas of clear colour, is hefty and hard-wearing and thus could be said to have some of the characteristics of tapestry, which is very hard-wearing indeed.

15. The tapestry weave construction made in double carpet wool.

16. The tapestry weave construction made in rug wool.

### How to Weave a Tapestry Bag

With a piece of plain paper, cut a pattern for the bag. The one measurement will be that which is from pins to pins, i.e. about 680mm (27in). The other will be whatever is a pleasant proportion for the bag when 680mm (27in) is folded into two. The illustrated bag in fig 17 is 340mm × 300mm (13½in × 11½in).

Now design a simple stripe design on the paper pattern, either with a pencil or the like or with strips of coloured paper or as described on page 82. The two sides of the bag need not be the same design. The illustrated bag has both sides the same, each side with three broad stripes of ochre or cinnamon colour each 90mm (3½in) wide, broken by two 38mm (1½in) stripes of white, each with a black stripe in the middle.

Set a string warp on the frame to the width of the bag and in the middle of the frame. For the weft you need two or three colours of rug wool or carpet wool. Rug wool is easily available and makes an excellent tapestry for the beginner, producing an even and satisfactory effect (see the white stripe in figs 16 and 17). Carpet wool (the wool used in carpet mills to produce the pile in carpets) used double is

17. The finished tapestry bag.

also excellent but produces a harsher and less even texture (see the darker stripes in figs 15 and 17). If carpet wool is not available in the shops, it can be obtained from suppliers or, if you live near a carpet town, from the mills and warehouses. If you really cannot obtain either of these (preferably the rug wool) and are raring to go, harsh double-knitting wool used double is a reasonable but expensive substitute.

Wind shuttles with the colours to be used. Rug wool is used singly, carpet wool and double-knitting wool both used double. Start weaving as described before. This time do not insert paper but weave right down to the panel pins. Insert each weft pick in an even larger arc than before, remembering what the weft has to do (look again at fig 9). In the illustrated bag, to weave a width of 300mm (11½in) each weft pick when held straight measured 350mm (13¾in). Pack the weft down firmly so that it entirely covers the warp. You will no doubt find at first that because the weft goes in so loosely you may get untidy loops of yarn at the selvedges and in the cloth – but put all your effort at this point in getting a near-perfect weave: weft totally covering the warp, all warp ends remaining absolutely straight and parallel with each other (no 'waisting') with neat, tidy and straight selvedges. If you can weave such a cloth on a simple frame like this with no mechanical aids you can truly say you are a weaver and you will have mastered a most important skill.

Weave with the same colour until your drawn design tells you it is time for a colour change. Cut off the yarn several centimetres away, pass it round the end warp and weave it back in the same shed for 25mm (1in) tucking the end to the back to be cut off later. Start your next colour in the same manner, and weave on, making further colour changes when necessary. If colour changes are some distance apart, end and start in this way, but if close together the yarns can be carried up the side of the weaving instead of being cut off (bind the unused thread in at the side with the weaving thread). If you run out of yarn while weaving join by overlapping for 25mm (1in) at the side.

Weave until the bottom of the bag is reached, i.e. the middle of the warp. Now make a row of knotted tufts as described on page 29. Continue weaving the other side of the bag right up to the far panel pins. If you find it hard to stretch so far the frame can be turned around and the weaving continued so, but you will have to beat the yarn into place with an upwards movement instead of a natural downwards movement. As you get near to the pins the shed-stick will have to be dispensed with and the last few picks can only be put in by removing the whole bag from the frame and darning the yarn in with a bodkin or weaving needle. These last few picks are critical to the neatness of the bag. It is very easy to pull the weaving in at this stage so take your time. This done, you now have the bag which, when folded, has a fringe at the bottom. Cut off any ends which are at the back of the cloth and trim the fringe.

### How to Make the Bag

The simplest way to make up the bag is to sew up both sides with the same colour yarn as the bag. It can be sewn on the right or on the wrong side. If your edges are not as neat as they might be then sew it on the wrong side. A sewing machine makes a good, neat and firm job, but take care with the stitch tension. The bag does not need lining but you can line it if you wish, either with lining material or, if its purpose requires, with plastic lining.

For the handle, make a good, thick, firm multi-stranded plait of the main colour yarn. The plait can be sewn on as it is but however firmly you have made it, when there are articles in the bag and it is slung over the shoulder the plait will inevitably stretch. This can be obviated by sewing it to some firm upholsterer's braid before attaching it to the bag. The bag is seen in fig 17.

Obviously bags can be of varied shapes and sizes. Tapestry also makes a good envelope-type bag.

Exactly the same weave-technique can be employed for making upholstery fabric (chair and stool seats), small flat floor mats and many other objects which need to be decorative, warm, firm, solid and hard-wearing.

# 5 Pile Rugs made on the Frame

**The Long Pile Rug**

String the frame as usual, right across the whole width of pins, *but* this time thread the shed-stick over *two* warp ends and under *two*. For the weft you need jute garden twine once more, natural colour, thick and soft if possible. This is for the rug ground-weave and is wound double on a shuttle-stick. You also need carpet yarn again. This time it *must* be carpet yarn or thick rug wool. Double knitting will *not* do. Buy the yarn in whole or broken skeins, in one or two colours.

Weave 25mm (1in) of tapestry in the doubled jute weft, with the warp working double. The shed-stick has been threaded 'over two and under two' and therefore when you thread the shuttle-stick through from the right, this must also be threaded 'under two, over two'. This doubling of the warp and weft means that the cloth weaves more quickly. Do not concern yourself too much if the jute weft does not cover the string warp entirely, this is basically a tapestry ground but it is not seen.

Now prepare the weft-tufts. The rug in figs 18 and 20 has a 75mm (3in) pile and the tufts were cut of carpet wool 175mm (7in) in length. Six strands at a time were used, three of orange and three of magenta, making a tuft of twelve. The length and the density of the pile is variable, so is the colour mixture. The six strands could all be of one colour, but remember that two close-toned reds mixed together make a more glowing red than just one. If thick rug wool is being used, put two strands together instead of six, making a tuft of four.

Cut your tufts by wrapping the wool around a stick or box which has a circumference of 175mm (7in). Cutting the wool with a razor blade or very sharp knife will be easier and will give a cleaner edge than using scissors. Prepare a quantity of pile at a time.

Now, with six (or two) strands of 175mm (7in) length wool, held in both hands, place the tuft across any two warp threads

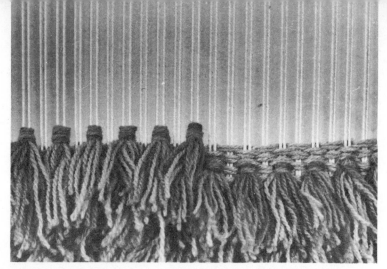

18. The weaving edge of the pile rug on the frame.

19. The Turkish knot.
20a. The finished pile rug.
20b. Detail of the finished pile rug.

which are working together and bring the two lots of ends round the back of and up through the middle of the two warps (see fig 19). This is a 'Turkish knot'. Pull it down snugly and produce similar tufts on every second doubled warp right across the rug (fig 18).

Weave another 25mm (1in) of jute tapestry ground. Make another row of tufts but this time on the doubled warps which were ignored on the last row of tufts.

Continue in this manner, taking care as usual to keep the warp ends straight and parallel by putting the jute weft in fairly slackly and thereby preventing 'waisting'.

Continue, as you did with the bag, right to the furthest panel pins, finishing with 25mm (1in) of jute and putting the last picks in with the aid of a large needle, bodkin or weaving needle (see Suppliers). If you find this last bit of weaving tedious you can finish before reaching the pins, as long as you sew along the last pick of jute, taking the needle and cotton through the warp's ends, to ensure there will be no unweaving. If you do this, when you take the rug-piece from the frame, sew back the unwanted bits of warp.

Take the rug-piece from the frame, give it a good shake to enliven the pile and throw it on the floor. You have an excellent piece of rug which will wear (and wash) for a *very* long time. Decide what size you want the total rug to be and weave more pieces accordingly. Sew these together at the back. No more need be done, your rug is complete. (see fig 20a).

## Other Rug Variations

### A Simple Graphic Design

The most obvious and rewarding variation is to make free graphic designs. Because the tufts are put in separately one at a time there is no need for them to be all the same colour. For instance, if you want a yellow circle on an orange ground on your rug, cut the rug out in newspaper, draw a circle on it and cut the newspaper up into pieces the size you can weave. You then draw, with a black felt pen, the shape that you will need on each small warp. Tuft with yellow in the circle areas and orange in the ground areas and join the pieces together. This is a simple concept and could be much more elaborate. However, there is often no need to be too elaborate. A simple design is often the most effective.

### Graduated Colour change

The next variation, again arising from the fact that the tufts are put in singly, is graduated colour change. Your rug could be white in the centre moving outwards through pale yellow, yellow, to oranges and a final glowing red at the edges. The rug could be striped or chequered, or any other design you desire.

### Cut and Looped Pile

The pile could be a short one, instead of long. Another variation is areas of cut and loop pile.

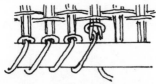

21. Making the Turkish knot over sticks.

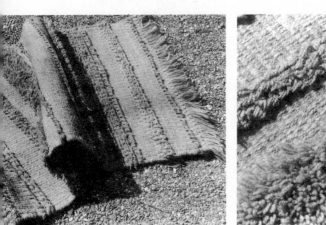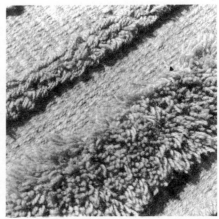

22. A rug composed of flat tapestry and cut and looped pile, total and detail.

The loop pile is achieved like this. Acquire two sticks of the width that you wish the length of the pile to be. Their length is unimportant but they must be smooth. Wind the strands for tufting into a small ball, i.e. do *not* cut into lengths. Place the two sticks along the weaving edge, holding them in the left hand, and make the looped knots over them as in fig 21. Withdraw the sticks when necessary and continue on along the row. This produces a row of loops. An interesting variation is to leave some loops and cut some. This is done by drawing a razor blade or sharp knife along and between the sticks where the cut pile is required. In fig 22 is a rug composed of flat tapestry, and looped and cut pile.

Rugs made in the above manner are almost indestructible. Wool and jute are two very sound, natural hard-wearing materials. They will be slow to soil, as wool is very dirt-resistant, but when they do finally become dirty, wash them in the bath in the gentle manner you would use with a woollen sweater, rinse well and dry in the open air, shaking well occasionally. Added to this if, after some years, the pile is trimmed at the very ends of the tufts with some extremely sharp scissors, the rug will look as new.

# 6 Weaving with Unspun Fleece

## Acquiring the Raw Material

This is a project especially interesting for those who live in or near the country, though the necessary materials can also be purchased (see Suppliers).

The weft material which produces the main texture is unspun fleece. If you are in the country during shearing time (May and June) you should be able to obtain fleeces at a very reasonable price. The price will depend upon the quality of the fleece, but, for this purpose, fleeces too harsh to be wanted by the clothing manufacturers are very satisfactory. In sheep farming areas you will be able to locate the farmer and ask if he has fleeces and is willing to sell. Fleeces come in a range of natural colours from creamy-white through greys to browns. The so-called 'black sheep' is really dark brown, and almost nobody but the individual craftsman wants his coat because dark fleeces are of less commercial value as they cannot be bleached or dyed (except black). Their only use is in army blankets. If you have the chance, buy two or three fleeces in various colours (a farmer will not sell part of a fleece).

Another method of obtaining your material is to gather the fleece from the hedges and fences where the sheep leave generous portions of their coats but for this you will need time to gather sufficient.

The final method is to order (generally by the kilo) from suppliers (see suppliers list).

## Preparing the Raw Material

You will need an overall to protect your clothes from grease and dirt during this operation. If you have bought a fleece from a farmer you must gently untie and unroll it, when you will find that it opens out to be animal shape again. The form of the fleece is little disturbed during shearing. The wool will certainly be greasy and probably dirty, although not too dirty as sheep are dipped some days prior to shearing. Do not be put off by the grease, it is pure lanolin, and handling fleece is very good for your hands. The dirt is another matter. First remove any obvious lumps of mud and rubbish which will be mainly around the edges of the fleece, particularly around the tail and back legs. Then sort the fleece. You will find that the fleece on the animal's back is softer and finer than that from around his legs and stomach for instance. Also, the colour will vary. With the sorted fleece in piles, choose the desired pile and 'tease' the fleece. This is opening out the fibres to allow particles of dirt to fall away. Do it over a white surface and you will see this happening. Take a handful of fleece in your left hand and, with the right hand, using the full length of palms and thumbs pull away a few fibres from the mass – and more – and more. The dirt will drop away all the while. When the mass in the right hand is a fair size put it somewhere clean and continue.

When you have a big pile of teased fleece, wash this very gently (squeezing not rubbing) in warm, soapy water, rinsing well and drying gently. You now have a mass of clean wool fibres with which to weave.

**Weaving a Pile Cushion Cover**

Although weaving with unspun fleece has many applications, for the sake of variation I suggest you now try a series of cushion covers.

Decide on the size of cover that you want, remembering that a cushion cover should be a fraction smaller than the actual cushion in order to make the cushion plump although shrinkage will generally take care of this factor. Make the warp on the frame according to the width of your cushion, allowing for turnings. This time do not use a stiff string but a lighter cotton string, dishcloth or 'health-vest' cotton doubled. Wind a shuttle-stick with thick white rug wool or double carpet wool. Starting right down at the pins, weave eight picks in a weave something between plain weave and tapestry, one over one under. Make a row of tufts, as described on page 29, but with tufts of fibre from the cleaned and washed wool. Continue in this manner, eight picks of rug wool, one row of fibre tufts until the desired amount for the cover has been woven. Lift the warp ends from the pins and knot them at the weaving edge. Take the weaving from the frame and give it a good shake. Weave the other side of the cushion cover in the same manner or in plain

23. Three cushions. 1 Rectangular cushion woven with tufts of fleece.
    2 Circular cushion woven with tufts of fleece and tufts of carpet wool.
    3 Square cushion woven with slubs of fleece.
24a. Close-up of the slub cushion cover.
24b. Close-up of the pile cushion covers.

weave and sew the two together, putting a zipper in one side. The
rectangular cushion in figs 23 and 24b was woven with tufts of
'black', grey and white fleece.

**Weaving a Slub Cushion Cover**

Make the warp as before and to your measurement requirements. Prepare a shuttle of white rug wool or doubled carpet wool. Weave six picks of firm, plain weave with this. Now draw from the fleece a big 'slub' of fibre, i.e. a mass of fibre, very thick in the centre and tapering off at both ends. Insert this into the weft in a shed-stick opening. Pull it up into loops in the thick centre, letting it tail off to flat and thin at the ends. Complete a *whole* pick in this manner. Weave three picks of white rug wool. Continue in this manner, one pick of fleece slubs, three picks of rug wool, finishing off with six picks of rug wool at the end of the cushion. Remove the cushion from the frame, knot off the spare warp ends. Weave the same again, or plain weave, for the other side of the cushion. Make the cover up with a zipper at one side.

The square cushion in fig 23 and in fig 24 was woven with slubs of 'black', grey and light grey fleece.

**Weaving a Circular Mixed-pile Cushion Cover**

Make a warp as before. Lay your circular cushion, or a paper pattern, on the warp and draw round it with a felt pen. With the help of plates of two sizes, draw two more concentric circles within this. Draw the whole thing on the portion of warp nearest to you. You will waste some warp at the far end but this cannot be avoided. Now, weaving in straight picks, but with each pick only weaving as far as the edge of the circle, weave six picks of white rug wool or doubled carpet wool. Insert a row of wool fibre tufts black in the outer circle, grey in the inner. Continue so until you reach the edge of the innermost circle when, in this circle, you make tufts of wool yarn instead of wool fibre. Finish the circle, knot off the extra warp all round the circle and cut away the rubbish. Weave another side the same, or plain weave. Make up the cushion.

The round cover in figs 23 and 24a was woven with tufts of 'black' and grey fleece and white carpet wool.

**Other Possibilities**

A flat neck-cushion cover can be woven by using the first or second techniques, weaving the whole of the warp available and folding the resulting cloth in two. Obviously there are many other cushion variations.

A very satisfactory object to make on the cushions principle (i.e. soft) but with pieces sewn together, is a knee-rug, or throw-over, or even a bed cover.

A shaped jacket or waistcoat could be made by following the principle of cushion 3 (i.e. weaving to a shape), thus obviating cutting.

Cushions were produced for this book in order to promote variation in the objects made, but very satisfactory rugs can be made by all three techniques used in the cushions but with a firm ground weave of hefty string or with a jute warp and tapestry weft. The pieces are then sewn together.

With the firm jute tapestry weft the techniques produce quite startling shoulder-bags.

# 7 More about Tapestry Weaving

If you refer back to chapter 4, you will see that various points emerged about tapestry: that the weft totally covers the warp; that tapestry is woven with a well-spaced cotton, linen or jute warp and a closely packed and loosely inserted wool weft; that rug wool makes a very good, smooth tapestry for the beginner, doubled carpet wool coming a close second but making a more textural effect; that you can obtain clear colour and areas of clear colour; that it is easy to make very effective horizontally striped designs of all sorts of complexity; and, finally, that tapestry is very hard-wearing and tough.

But many other things are possible and some of these I now suggest you explore in a 'sampler' – work not intended to be anything but an experiment and an exploration into just how far one can push a technique (fig 25).

Set on the usual string warp. Prepare the wool weft by choosing two good colours with which you enjoy working – and carry out the following design exercises. The samples photographed were woven in olive green and ice blue.

## Design Stemming Naturally From Tapestry Technique

1  Weave 25mm (1in) in colour A and two picks in B. Repeat this three times (fig 26). The object of this exercise is to show you how to make fine, horizontal lines. Making a line of one pick would not work, it would appear as a line of spots (see fig 29).

2  Weave one pick of colour A and one of B. Continue so for 50mm (2in). We now have vertical lines (fig 27). If at intervals two different picks are put in of the same colour, the vertical lines of colour will change places.

3  Weave 25mm (1in) as exercise 2 and 25mm (1in) of two picks of colour A and two picks of colour B. Repeat all this once. You now have patterning composed of vertical and horizontal lines (fig 28).

25. The whole tapestry sampler.

26. Tapestry weaving, close-up of horizontal lines.
27. Tapestry weaving, close-up of vertical lines.
28. Tapestry weaving, vertical and horizontal lines.

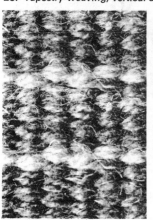 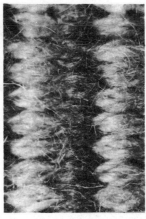 

29. Tapestry weaving, small 'spot' pattern.

30. Tapestry weaving, larger 'spot' pattern.

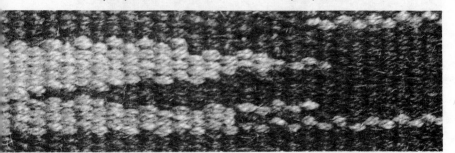

31. Tapestry weaving, free patterning, random meeting points.

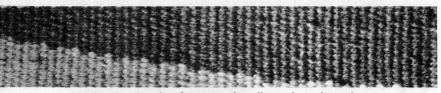

32. Tapestry weaving, free patterning, diagonal meeting points.

33. Tapestry weaving, free patterning, curved meeting points.

4   Weave seven picks of colour A and one of colour B. Repeat this six times and you have a small spot pattern (fig 29).

5   Weave five picks of colour A, one of B, one of A and one of B. Repeat all this six times and you have a stronger spot pattern (fig 30).

All the above exercises have a geometric quality about them and are capable of infinite variation to form further designs and repeat patterns.

## Making Free Graphic Shapes

1   Weave colour A in from the left and bring the shuttle out of the shed and to the surface of the tapestry at any point. In the same shed bring colour B in from the right, weave up to A and bring the shuttle to the surface of the tapestry. In the next shed, weave both colours back to their respective selvedges. Repeat these two picks, varying the meeting-point of the colours every time. This will give you two areas of clear colour melding in a random fashion (fig 31).

2   With the same two colours you could now make a more clear-cut change of colour. On the first two picks make the colours meet 25mm (1in) from the right of the work. For the subsequent 25mm (1in) of weaving make each meeting point two warp ends to the left; for the next 25 mm (1in) four warp ends to the left and for the next 25mm (1in) eight warp ends to the left. You will have produced two areas of clear colour meeting at three different angles (fig 32).

3   Draw a quarter circle on the warp with a felt pen, or cut a paper pattern and follow it. This method creates two areas of colour whose meeting creates a curve (fig 33). When you have done this you will realize that as soon as the angle of meeting becomes very vertical, slits in the tapestry occur. This is called 'khelim weaving' and has been exploited to great advantage both in traditional and in modern tapestries.

4   Pursuing the 'slit' idea, weaving as before, bring colour A in from the left and B in from the right to meet in the dead centre of the tapestry, continue in this manner and you will have a slit right down the middle which literally divides the tapestry area in two. Make sure that the two edges meet each other exactly and neatly (fig 34).

5   Weave as for 4 but before allowing each colour to return to its own selvedge, twist the two colours around one another once. This will close the slit and return the tapestry to one piece (fig 35). This should be woven very precisely and neatly.

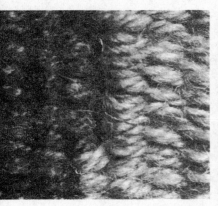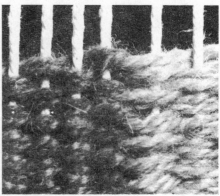

34. Tapestry weaving, vertical meeting point forming a slit.
35. Tapestry weaving, vertical meeting point joined.

6   Draw a circle or a rectangle on the warp with another circle or rectangle inside it. Prepare not shuttles but 'butterflies' (see page 15) of both colours. Weave each colour in the appropriate place (fig 36), weaving one entire pick, though composed of several separate areas of colour, at once, and pressing it into place. When starting a colour in, just bring it in from the back leaving the end hanging. With a complex tapestry which has a great deal of figuring (and therefore many butterflies of yarn and many yarn ends where figures begin and end) the tapestry should be woven face-down so that all the 'rubbish' is uppermost. It does not look good while you are weaving but it is quicker.

7   In all the weaving we have done, the weft has always been put

36. Tapestry weaving, free patterning, a double rectangle.

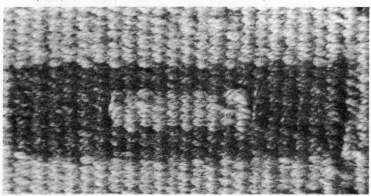

37. Tapestry weaving, curving and shaped wefts.

in one *total* pick at a time, on the horizontal, and the whole horizontal pick pressed into place at once. If we so desire, from a design point of view, this is not absolutely essential. Draw a waving design on your warp with a felt pen and follow the shapes and lines with the weft (see fig 37).

### Suggestions for Projects – Bags, Rugs and a Wallhanging

If you have tried all these ideas, you will by now have learned a great deal more about tapestry weaving and it would be interesting to make another bag, but with a design composed of some of the things in the sampler. As a beginner, choose selectively. When designing, never put too much in or the impact of the design is lost. A bag in red and orange with a simple circle on a ground would look well; or a bag based on the sea, woven in greens and turquoise and using technique 7 would be pleasant.

If you like flat rugs then you could now weave a quite complex design, but your edges must be woven impeccably so that the joins will sew together well.

Another very pleasant thing to make, depending upon your personal inclination, would be a piece of pure decoration, with no function except to be aesthetically pleasing. Fig 38 shows a wallhanging produced on the frame using most of the tapestry techniques described, together with tufting. If you examine the photograph you will see that the hanging incorporates tufting, plain and striped tapestry, fine lines, vertical lines, slits, colour areas, spotted areas,

38. Tapestry weaving, wallhanging encompassing many of the foregoing techniques. Irene Waller.

random melding, weft deviating from the horizontal and 'warp wrapping' – something not dealt with specifically here but which is merely the production of tapestry on as few as two warp ends only.

This wallhanging also introduces the idea of more abstract design and intent. The purpose of a wallhanging is to give visual pleasure and intellectual stimulation and this requires something more than materials and technique – some sort of personal vision which is worth transmitting to others. This wallhanging has trees, branches and growth as the source of its shapes and textures, but the general idea was to produce a piece of work which 'hung' and had a feeling of broken verticality, increasing in weight towards the bottom. Fig 39 is 'Phase'. A tapestry produced by the New York artist Susan Weitzmann. Fig 40 is an immense tapestry hanging in a hotel in Kansas City. It was produced in sections and is weighted with stones.

39. 'Phase' Black and white tapestry, Susan Weitzmann, New York.

One only attempts work of this sort if an idea is burning in one's brain. It is not a therapy, as producing an area of plain weaving can be – too much constant thought and creative effort has to go into it.

It is excellent if you can work with the frame on an easel, as a painter would. Thus you have it placed at the angle at which the work is finally to be seen; you can stand well back from it to judge how it is progressing and it can remain vertical and undisturbed while it is in progress.

Some of the mechanics of designing are discussed in chapter 13.

# 8 A Freer Concept

The wallhanging in fig 38 is an attempt to communicate some abstract idea, however simple, to the onlooker. Figs 39, 40, 45 and the frontispiece are all very impressive pieces of work by internationally known artists.

You may very soon, therefore, wish to free yourself of the restraint of the rectangular frame. Another method is to acquire a 'frame' of a size and shape which interests you and which will remain part of the finished piece of work. In fig 41 a metal hoop was used, and in fig 44 a tree branch.

## The Circular Tapestry

Acquire or make a metal, wood or plastic hoop. It must not be too bulky in itself and it must be perfectly round and flat. A very large lampshade ring is ideal. Cut thirty-two lengths of string or jute twine, each one at least one and a half times the diameter of the circle. Knot the first one across the hoop, bisecting it. Use a simple knot, easy to undo, and leave the same amount of waste yarn at each end (fig 42). Knot the second thread across the loop at right angles to the first, bisecting it again. Knot the third thread across the hoop between threads one and two and the fourth in the remaining space. Knot four more threads across the loops in the spaces left by the first four. Knot eight threads across in the spaces thus created. Knot sixteen in the remaining spaces. You now have an equally spaced radiating 'warp' of sixty-four ends knotted on to the hoop. Undo one knot and take this individual end back to the centre, knotting it there and pushing the end to the back. Ease the surrounding warp ends to fill in the gap. Result: sixty-three ends. An odd number of warp ends is essential in circular and thus continuous weaving.

Prepare a shuttle, weaving needle, big bodkin or 'butterfly' of

40. Massive tapestry wallhanging in a hotel in Kansas City, total and detail, designed by Evelyn Anselvicius and woven in Mexico.

weft yarn. The weft yarn in fig 41 is jute and in fig 43 is sometimes wool and sometimes jute. Start weaving, one over one under, from as near the centre as you can get. Make sure you are weaving in the dead centre and not off centre. The centre will not look very decorative at this stage but ignore it for the moment. When the weaving is started and established you must consider the design. Obviously this must be based on radiating forms. Fig 41 was again based on branches and twigs, but the sun, starfish, flowers, or ripples are all possible source material. If you wish, draw your design on paper and place it behind the work when you want to check. A drawn design is not essential since the work can progress very well without one. You will soon see why you knotted the warp ends on to the hoop individually instead of winding the warp on in one long, continuous thread as you did on the weaving frame. Where you want to produce curved shapes you will need to release a few warp ends to gain more length. Treat the knotted warp as being very flexible, tightening and loosening whenever and wherever necessary. Split the warp into areas, perhaps getting ever smaller. When you do this you will have to bring in more separate pieces of weft. The warp ends may well by now have lost their original equidistance completely. There is no need to weave in the same yarn or colour in all parts. Both can be varied.

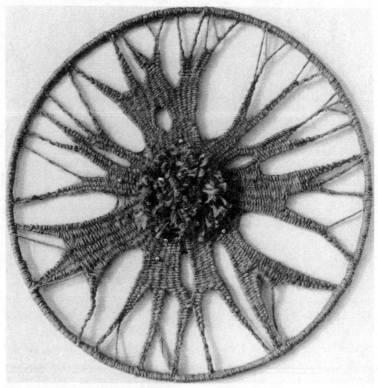

41. Circular tapestry. Irene Waller.

When all weft ends meet the hoop, secure for a moment with sellotape. Now with one thread bind the frame tightly and firmly, binding in a section of each warp and weft thread as you come to it. Only bind in enough of each thread to keep it secure, cut off the extra. Embellish the centre of the tapestry with tufts put in with a needle. Fibre, beads, and decorative wire etc can also be pleasing. Regard your product critically and from a distance and see if it pleases you. If it does not, apply some of the suggestions on page 80.

## A Three-dimensional Tapestry

Find a tree-branch with lots of shape and dimension to it. Branches with decorative bark, like silver or white birch, and lichened branches can be intriguing to work with. Gather together any interesting yarns, you will have by now collected, including sewing and embroidery threads. String tiny 'warps' across and through your branch, creating new dimensions. Weave into your warps wherever you feel it is visually desirable. You could add stones, beads or pebbles. The whole thing can be large or quite miniature. Spray the finished piece of work with a mixture of 50/50 PVA and

42. Knotting the warp on the circular frame.

43. Circular tapestries in progress in a class at the College of New Caledonia, Prince George, British Columbia.

water (see Suppliers) several times from a hair-spray canister or garden mister, and you will have a piece of stiff, solid 'sculpture' (see fig 44).

44. *(previous page)* Three-dimensional textile object fashioned on a tree-branch. Karin Vliegar, Rio de Janeiro.

## Other Possibilities

You are now weaving 'off the loom' and in a very free and creative manner. If this manner of working appeals to you, many other possibilities will suggest themselves. A piece of interesting driftwood can have random warps hanging from it, weighted with stones, shells or the beautiful pieces of sea-ground glass you can pick up on the beaches.

Two hoops could be put together like a gyroscope, creating a three-dimensional circular weaving.

Square and triangular frames could be interesting to work with, or two squares put together to form a three-dimensional shape.

The middle of a circular tapestry, such as that in fig 41, could be exaggerated and instead of being a pile of tufts could be the anchorage for yarns streaming down to a length of two or three feet, weighted with beads or not as you wish.

The possibilities are considerable, but this sort of work is just as likely to stem from first finding one's 'frame' and being inspired to work with it than from necessarily deciding that one is going to produce a certain manner of object. So, when in the garden, in the country, or on holiday, keep your eyes open.

# 9 Additions to the Frame Loom

**Advantages of the Loom as it is**

The practical advantages of the frame loom are that it is portable, light, easy to set up and uncomplicated to use. Its aesthetic advantages are that it takes one right into the essence of weaving as a procedure, with all its satisfactions and possibilities, without fuss, delay or expense. One of the most valid reasons for its use is, in my opinion, this instant entry into the essence of the weaving process with nothing standing between the weaver and the product. The fact that most of the interlacing of the weft into the warp is done very directly with the fingers and the simplest of tools, immerses the operator in the manipulation of threads and the making of a thread interlacement immediately. Magdalena Abakanowicz, who is a Polish artist using fibre, thread and the weave interlacement as her media, and undoubtedly one the greatest of such artists now practising, works in this manner – direct involvement with the piece of work, however large, by interlacing weft into warp with her fingers thus achieving intense involvement with every square inch of her product. 'However large' is, when speaking of Abakanowicz' work, a provocative comment, see 'Woven Wall' (fig 45).

True weaving can be achieved with minimal mechanical aid. If you have succeeded in establishing such sensitivity to the warp and weft that you can weave a piece of rectangular cloth with straight edges and even texture, without mechanical assistance, you can be well satisfied with the achievement. Many people desire to work in no other manner. If, on the other hand, anything short of perfection has been achieved, with consequent dissatisfaction, then first look back and read again the instructions on page 21, or if that does not satisfy then resort to some of the additions to the loom now dealt with, which both speed weaving up and assist in keeping straight selvedges.

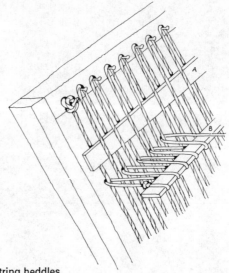

46.  Making string heddles.

## The Addition of String Heddles to Speed Weaving

The shed-stick (A) when turned on end gives one opening or 'shed' through which the weft passes on every second pick. On every other pick the weft has had to be threaded through end by end.

   A second mechanical shed can be achieved by the addition of string heddles and is done thus:– you need a small ball of fine, soft, strong string or twine, a second shed-stick (B) and some sellotape. The heddles are made when the warp is on the frame and shed-stick A has been inserted. Ask a helper to stand or sit at the back of the frame, facing you, and to hold shed-stick B 75mm (3in) above the warp and midway between the near panel pins and shed-stick A, which can be pushed back. Tie the string to stick B immediately above either of the selvedges of the warp. Now take the string down and around the warp end which lies below stick A, up over stick B, down around the next warp end lying below stick A, over B and so on, catching all the warp ends which lie below stick A in individual 75mm (3in) loops of string which all pass around stick B. Work to the end, taking care to keep all the loops very even, and tie off. Now

45.  *Previous page*: 'Woven Wall', Magdalena Abakanowicz, Poland. A massive textile wall produced entirely in plain weave and with the fingers, with little mechanical aid.

run a piece or pieces of sellotape right across the loops where they pass over stick B, very firmly so that they cannot move.

You now have a second mechanized shed which is made by lifting stick B when required. The loops and stick B lie on the face of the warp when not needed. The effect of a second mechanical shed is to speed up weaving somewhat.

## Use of a Reed to Control the Width of the Cloth

A reed is a warp-spacer and looks like a large, fine comb closed on both long sides (fig 47); these were originally made of reeds, hence their name. A reed cannot be made with ease and should be obtained from suppliers. It must be as wide as the warp but narrower than the inside of the frame-loom and when ordered you must specify how many spaces you require per 25 mm(1in) (we have been using four) and the desired length of the reed. While the warp is being wound on to the pins, the reed is placed within the frame, across the width, and each warp end is passed through a space in the reed before being settled on its pin. When all is done, the reed is seen to be settled within the frame, controlling the placing of each warp end. It is brought down to near the fell (weaving-edge) of the cloth as each weft pick is pressed into place to facilitate keeping the edges of the weaving straight and each warp end in its own place. Use of the reed does not obviate the necessity for leaving large arcs of weft yarn to avoid pulling-in. Remember that the reed can only be released from the frame by cutting the warp ends so do not use one if you are planning to weave to the very end to utilize the natural looping of the warp ends as suggested for the bag (page 28).

## The Use of Reed and Heddles Together

If you furnish your warp with string heddles and a reed then you are both speeding up weaving and keeping a watch on the cloth width and warp-thread emplacement. However, by the time you have got to this point a simpler way of doing the same thing is to use a rigid heddle which takes the place of three things, shed-stick A, shed-stick B and a reed.

47.  The reed, close-up.

## The Use of the Rigid Heddle to Speed Weaving and Control Width

A rigid heddle is obtainable from suppliers and is so-called because it is a series of heddles (metal this time, not string, and more complex) held rigidly in a frame (fig 48).

Like the reed, it must be as wide as the warp but narrower than the inside of the frame. Unlike reeds, heddles do not come in a wide variety of spacings. They generally accommodate twelve warp ends to 25mm (1in), but you can find out from the supplier's catalogue.

So you either have to re-position the panel pins and have six warp ends per 25mm (1in) instead of four, or make a closer cloth with twelve ends per 25mm (1in), or make some other mathematical adjustment. Like the reed, the rigid heddle is placed within the frame and the warp string is passed through it during the process of warping the frame. But this time one warp end passes through a hole, the next, through a space, and so on. When all is done, if the heddle is lifted,

48. The rigid heddle, close-up.

it gives one shed and if lowered the other, and if brought down to near the fell of the cloth, it acts as a warp-spacer. Remember that, like the reed, the rigid heddle must be cut from the warp.

# 10 The Rigid Heddle Loom

### The Loom and its Advantages

The rigid heddle loom (fig 49) is one of the simplest looms proper that there is. It has two main advantages over the frame. Firstly, it can produce greater area of cloth or larger objects without recourse to joining. (Rigid heddle looms can take up to about 3½m (4 yards) of average weight warp and come in various widths up to 20in (508mm).) Secondly, the loom has within it the mechanisms for making both sheds, for warp spacing, and for pressing the weft into place if the cloth is a light-weight one (for tapestry one would still use a fork or a tapestry beater). Also, it is not an expensive item of equipment. *However*, the rigid heddle has twelve or thirteen spaces to the inch (25mm) and therefore one's choice of warp is limited to three-ply knitting wool thickness and less.

But, assuming that one wishes to make bigger pieces of *cloth* without necessarily going into greater complexity of cloth structure (for which one needs four-shaft looms and upwards, see chapter 14), then a rigid heddle loom can be a simple and inexpensive purchase. For this you will need the suppliers' catalogues.

49. The rigid heddle loom.

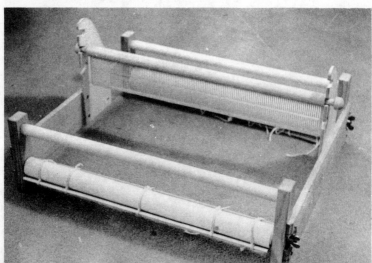

I am assum... you have the loom in front of you and I propose to follow the ...nique as with the frame: to outline a series of specific a... ...imple projects to follow through step by step.

First you ... d the principle and making of the warp because this proce... ...ommon to all projects. On a weaving frame the warp was ... as a continuous thread between the panel pins. Now imag... to be $3\frac{1}{2}$m (4 yards) long instead of 710mm (28in) long... ...d heddle loom will not be $3\frac{1}{2}$m (4 yards) long, it will be ab... mm (18in) from front to back. However, it is equipped with ro... So you will make your warp not on the loom but like a long $3\frac{1}{2}$m ... yards) skein. You will then spread it out width-wise and roll it on to the loom as a flat cylinder of thread. The precedure is as follows:

## Making the Warp

First decide upon the size of your object. It must obviously be within the loom's limits. (You can contemplate joining again and then you could make big areas of cloth like curtains and bedcovers.) As an example for warping, take the first object dealt with in chapter 12, i.e. a wrap, 450mm (18in) wide and 2·2m (7 feet) long.

You must now determine the length of the warp and the number of threads in the warp. The length is the length of the object; 2·2m (7 feet), plus shrinkage, 150mm (6in), plus loom wastage, 620mm (2 feet), plus extra warp for weaving experimentation (optional, but could be, 310mm (1 foot) or 620mm (2 feet); you can ignore it in this instance). Thus the length is 2·2m (7 feet) plus 150mm (6in) plus 620mm (2 feet) = 2·9m (9 feet 6in). The number of ends in the warp is the width of the object, 450mm (18in), plus shrinkage, 50mm (2in), multiplied by the number of ends per 25mm (1in) which is determined by the heddle itself (in this case twelve, i.e. six holes and six spaces.) (When using metric measurements divide by 25.) Then add four extra threads for strengthening the selvedges (two at either side). Thus the total number of warp ends will be 450mm + 50mm, i.e. 500mm, $\times \frac{12}{25} = 240, +4 = 244$. (In Imperial units, 18in + 2in, i.e. 20, $\times 12 = 240, +4 = 244$.) So you need to make your warp 2·9m (9 feet 6in) long and it must have 244 ends in it.

The warp thread is made by winding it on posts of some sort. The simplest and cheapest way is to drive some huge nails into something 2·9m (9 feet 6in) apart with a third nail 230mm (9in) away from one of the end ones. Or you can make the warp on stool-legs if you wedge two stools firmly upside down. However, the correct weaving equipment for making simple warps is either a set of warping posts or a warping board. Both are obtainable from suppliers or can be made by a carpenter (figs 50 and 51).

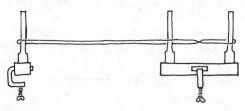

50. Warping posts.

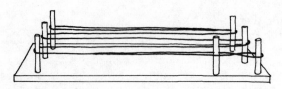

51. A warping board.

So, assuming you have acquired your nails or stool-legs or posts or board, you wind the 2·9m (9 feet 6in) 'skein' either straight or zigzagged as follows. Make a loop in the end of the warp thread, measure off 2·9m (9 feet 6in), put a pin in the yarn at that point. Arrange the posts so that you can wind a warp of this length. Loop the warp thread to one post, take the thread the 2·9m (9 feet 6in) distance where there must be two posts. Cross it around these posts as in fig 50 and take it back. You have made two of your warp threads with a 'cross' at one end. The purpose of the cross is to keep each thread in its own place. Continue in this manner to make your 244 threads, ending off at the same post which you started with. While warping, tie the threads in bundles of ten or twenty so that you won't lose count. Warp carefully, controlling tension. Do not have the yarn too tight or too sloppy and keep the same tension from beginning to end. If you have to join the yarn, do this at one of the ends, *never* in the middle.

Now take the two cross-sticks which come with the loom. (These will have holes at either end.) Insert them where the two posts are which have made the cross and tie them together 50mm (2in) apart, via the holes. Now remove the warp from the posts by chaining. This is done by crocheting the warp with the hands, starting at the post furthest from the cross. When near the cross and the sticks, take the whole warp from the equipment and place it on a table.

## Putting the Warp on the Loom

Tie the rigid heddle into the loom. Set the loom on the table with its back roller nearest to you. Settle the chained warp on the table beyond the loom with its cross-sticks between the front roller (furthest away from you) and the heddle.

Now observe where the warp ends go through the cross-sticks. One end goes over and under the sticks and the next under and over and both form a loop. Take the first loop and thread it through the furthest right-hand space of the heddle. The correct implement is a reed-hook or heddle hook (from suppliers), but a crochet hook will do. When the loop is through, place it on a warp-stick (supplied with the loom). Continue in this manner, threading the loops through the spaces of the rigid heddle, ignoring the holes. Make *very* sure that each time, you take the loop which is next in order and do not muddle them.

When all the loops are through the heddle, tie the stick on which they rest to the stick and linen on the back roller of the loom (nearest to you), securing the back roller with the wing-nut, or ratchet. Now turn the loom and warp around. Grasp the warp where it is undisturbed and shake it gently so that any warp ends disturbed in the threading shake back into place.

You are now ready to wind the warp onto the loom. You need lots of newspaper to do this, double, as wide as the back roller and enough to roll on with the entire warp. You also need the warp-sticks which come with the loom. The process of winding the warp onto the back roller of the loom is called beaming and, though ultimately a one-man job, at this stage if it can be done by two people it is very much easier. One person holds the loom, turns the roller, puts in the paper and sticks and secures the roller. The other holds the warp tightly, moving further down it all the time and moves the cross-sticks forward with it (they are always just in front of the heddle); but, most important of all, keeps the warp ends evenly at tension so that the warp ends go on to the back roller of the loom evenly, smoothly and tightly and in the shape of a straight cylinder (watch the edges to see that the end warps are well on the paper and sticks and do not slide off. The warp is wound on until the looped ends are level with the front of the loom.

Now transfer the cross from the front to the back of the heddle. Undo the ties at either ends of the cross-sticks. Grasp the warp firmly and turn the cross-stick nearest the heddle on end. Put another stick into the shed thus made on the *far* side of the heddle. Push it back and take out the original cross-stick. Now turn the remaining cross-stick on end. Put a cross-stick into the shed thus made on the far side of the heddle, taking out the original cross-stick. Replace the warp stick with a cross-stick tie the cross-sticks together. The cross is now at the back of the rigid heddle.

Cut all the loops at the front of the warp. Now re-thread the warp through the rigid heddle, one thread through a space, the next through a hole right the way across with two double threads at either edge. Refer to the order of the warp ends where they cross between the cross-sticks. When all the ends are threaded tie them on to the front stick of the loom in 25mm (1in) groups as the knot in fig 52. When all are done, close your eyes and run your fingers across the warp to test whether all warp ends are tied at the same tension. If not, correct them. When you are quite satisfied, tie a second knot. In order to start weaving the correct width of cloth, pull the two end knots outwards so that the selvedge warps are absolutely parallel.

Wind your chosen weft yarn on a shuttle-stick. Wind also some yarn of a contrasting colour to the warp onto a shuttle-stick and start to weave with this. The weaving method is as before except that you now lift and lower the heddle to get your sheds and press

52. The adjustable knot for tying on the warp.

the weft yarn into place with the heddle. Weave 25mm (1in) of the contrasting yarn while the groups of threads gradually spread out. This is the moment to look for errors in threading and to correct them if any are found.

Now start weaving with your chosen yarn.

If you find the loom light-weight, for instance if it lifts up when you lift the heddle, make some weighting arrangement. A brick with a string and a hook will do the job.

Should you feel that the restiction to comparatively finer warps than we have hitherto been using is a nuisance, then there are two-way or Tabby looms available which are more flexible. On them one can use a much wider variety of weights of yarn. They are more heavily constructed and therefore stay firmly in place. However, they are roughly three and a half times the price of a rigid heddle loom and if you are going to make this financial outlay then it may be preferable to invest in a four-shaft loom (chapter 14) which will allow greater complexity of cloth construction.

# 11 Weaving on the Rigid Heddle or Two-way Loom

## Weaving a Wrap

To weave a wrap suitable for day or evening wear, still with easily available materials, you will need some knitting wool or Dryad's Atherstone wool in two- or three-ply in white, natural, black or a colour. If you are using white, natural or black and have some white or black unspun fleece, you can use that too. Buy 250gm (8oz) wool at first – this will make the warp and start the weft. Measure how many centimetres (or inches) of weft 50gm or an once will weave and then you will know how much more to buy to complete the wrap.

To make a finished wrap 508mm (20in) by 2·2m (7 feet), make a warp according to the calculations in the last chapter, put it on to the loom and prepare to weave just as described. While you are weaving with the contrasting yarn at the beginning experiment also with the amount of arc required to get a perfect weave and a good selvedge.

Now with the correct weft yarn, weave six picks of doubled weft (basket-weave). To do this put one pick through, press it down, return the heddle to the same rest, put the weft back through the same shed but catch it around the end warp thread to prevent it coming unwoven. Then weave six picks of plain weave and one pick of gauze weave (fig 52a). Gauze weave is done from the right with the yarn on the shuttle. No shed is used but the warp ends are crossed over each other in doubled pairs (or any other number) as the weft-stick is inserted. Help this weft pick down with a fork. Now six picks of plain weave, six picks of basket and one pick of unspun fleece pulled up into loops, as you did the cushion (see page 36) but smaller. If you are using a colour, do this with several strands of wool instead of fleece. This is one repeat and the illustrated fabric in fig 53 was woven in this manner. Continue weaving until the

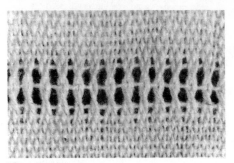

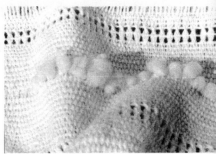

52a. Gauze weave.
53. Fabric for the woollen wrap. Stripes of plain weave, basket weave,
gauze weave and texture weave.

desired length is reached, finishing as you started. Hem-stitch or knot the threads at both ends of the warp. Take out the contrasting yarn, trim the fringes. Even with this simple weave design there are many variations. You could increase the amount and area of the gauze weaving and the texture weaving. You could introduce metallic yarns or weave with a self-colour mohair weft instead of plain wool.

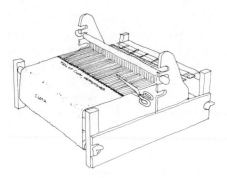

53a. Cutting weaving from the rigid heddle loom.

## Window Drapes

The weave suggested for window drapes (fig 54) is very effective and very economical in warp yarn and warp threading. It also makes excellent room dividers. An important factor is to choose the correct weft yarns. The principle is to put onto the loom three very narrow bands of warp side by side but with big spaces between them. Thus when the weft is put in, vast sections of weft yarn travelling horizontally will remain unwoven. When the resulting

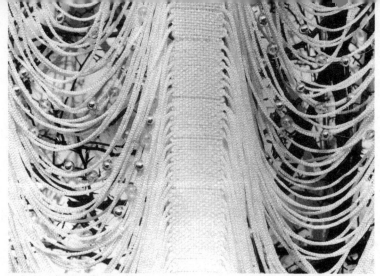

54. Window drape woven with spaced bands of warp. Weft of 'Novacord', and glass beads strung on nylon line.

'cloth' is taken from the loom and the bands brought nearer together and hung on a bar the wefts, if correctly chosen, will drape in very pleasing curves, hence the importance of choosing the correct weft yarn. Test the weft yarn by holding an 200mm (8in) length in both hands and letting it drape and curve; see whether it does this satisfactorily. Heavy silky yarns and chenilles are excellent.

First decide whether you wish to curtain one or several small windows (say 380mm (15in) wide), or whether you wish to join your cloth to curtain a larger aperture. If the former, make a warp of health-vest or dishcloth cotton of fifty-four ends and not longer than about 3·5m (4 yards). This will give you three 38mm (1½in) warp bands each with eighteen threads in it. If the latter, make the warp of forty-six ends to get one side and the middle band 38mm (1½in) wide and the other side band 20mm (¾in) wide. This will join on to a similar band in the next piece of weaving. When threading the warp through the heddle, thread only in the centre and two sides When beaming your warp, use plenty of stiff paper and warp sticks, otherwise the three narrow bands of warp threads will become sloppy and unmanageable.

When you are ready to weave, choose your weft yarn or yarns carefully for drape and curve. Make sure also that they look good with the light *behind* them. Wind these on to shuttles and wind also three 'butterflies' of the same yarn as the warp.

Begin by weaving with the three 'butterflies' on each warp band separately. Put each of the three wefts in, press down, next weft, press down and so on. Weave for 65mm (2½in) – this is to make a pocket-like hem to take a bar at the top or bottom of the curtain.

Now insert one weft proper, right across the warps – and a second. Now weave two picks with the 'butterflies' on each individual warp band. These four picks are the weave-repeat, i.e. two right across and two on each separate band. Continue until you have woven enough for your purpose. Weave another three 65mm (2½in) pocket-hems and either remove the piece from the loom or weave a second piece.

Make the hems, slip a bar in top and bottom (either wood, metal or perspex) and draw the warp bands together until a satisfactory curve is given to the unwoven wefts. The curtain in fig 54 was woven with a weft of 'Novacord' and glass beads strung on fishing-line. The technique was also incorporated in the wallhanging in fig 56.

## Texture-weaves for Cushions etc

The method of weaving now to be described is really a three- or four-shaft weave, i.e. it needs more variations than just the two sheds possible with the rigid heddle loom. However, it is quite possible to do it on the simpler loom.

The principle is to have a fairly firm, plain ground-weave of something like three-ply wool. However, in the warp, at intervals of about every 12mm (½in) there is set a fine, strong yarn. This yarn lies unused under, or incorporated in, the plain weave some of the time, and when required is brought to the face of the cloth where you insert under it all sorts of fancy wefts such as unspun fleece, braids, ribbons, bundles of yarn etc (see fig 55). It is then taken to the

55. Texture weave.

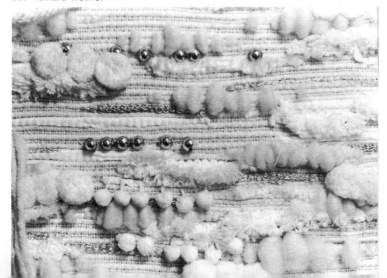

57. Detail of 56.

back of, or incorporated in, the cloth again until required. So, assuming you are making a cushion; make a warp of something like a three-ply wool at twelve ends per 25mm (inch). Now make a second warp, the same length but one-sixth of the number of threads in a sewing cotton or the like and in a contrasting colour. When both warps are made, chained and lying on the table ready for the first threading through the heddle, after you have threaded the woollen warp, place the cotton warp on top of it and thread one loop (two threads) through the heddle every 25mm (inch).

Beam both warps together. Thread the woollen warp through the heddle, as normal, then thread the cotton warp, one end through every sixth space. Tie on. When ready to weave, slide a stick between the two warps between the heddle and the cross-sticks so that when turned on end it will lift the fine cotton warps only. Thus you use the heddle, either up or down for the base-weave and the stick turned on end for when you wish to insert the fancy wefts (fig 55). This technique was also incorporated in the big wallhanging in fig 56.

Wallhanging, Irene Waller, 1974, for Dudley College of Education,

# 12 Further Possibilities of Plain Weave

Plain weave is the most stable and practical weave there is. Its aesthetic appeal may well lie in its structural simplicity, necessitating the extra careful choice of yarns and colour. Someone once said 'endeavour to make much with little' and here you are indeed doing so. The following are some of the variations available:

1    Basket weave – single warp, doubled weft.
2    Hopsack – double warp and double weft.
3    Grouped wefts – one, two, three or more wefts (fig 58), inserted into one shed.
4    Warp spacing (fig 54). Spacing can be as large as the illustration or as little as two threads.
5    Weft spacing (fig 59).
6    Warp and weft spacing together.

The above three techniques make open fabrics very suitable for curtains and light-weight wraps and scarves.

58. Grouped wefts, woven into a twisted or 'gauze' warp construction, Doreen Hope.
59. Weft spacing, with warp yarn variation in stripes.

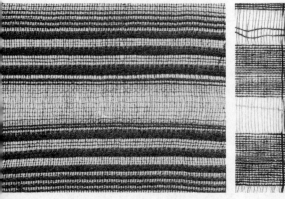
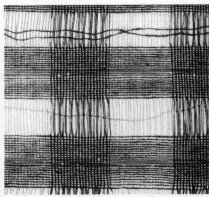

7  Warp colour striping – results in vertical stripes.

8  Weft colour striping – results in horizontal stripes.

9  Warp and weft colour spacing together – results in ginghams, checks and tartans.

7, 8 and 9 are suitable for clothing fabric.

10  Irregular placing of the weft. The weft is pushed into place with the fingers or by adjusting the angle of the heddle. This method has been used by some very great textile artists. The results are a little unstable and should be either held by spraying with a fixative solution like starch, or by inserting clear shapes of acetate (fig 60).

11  Fancy yarns of all descriptions, gimps, loops, chenilles etc give infinite variety of texture.

12  Weft yarn twisting. Two yarns of contrasting colours are wound onto the shuttle together and twisted before entering the shed. This gives a very dominant broken colour and broken textured effect (fig 61).

13  Weaving with beads. These are slung onto a needle threaded with the same yarn as the weft. The beaded weft is inserted when required and the beads manipulated into place before the weft is pressed down. They can be used in great quantity or occasionally as in fig 55.

60.  Irregular placing of the weft. Two weaves produced in a class held with the Kamalka Weavers, Vernon, British Columbia.

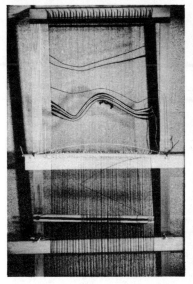
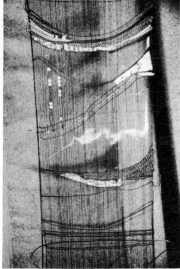

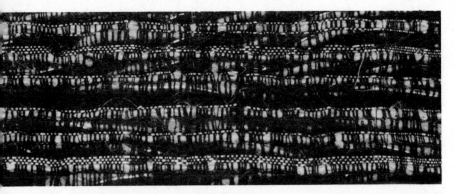

61. Weft yarn twisting, Patricia Keddie.

14   Weaving with ribbons. These can be inserted flat or crushed.

15   Weaving with fur. Strips of fur inserted as weft picks and linked perhaps with heavy woollen yarns of the same colour tones can make interesting cloth for jackets etc. Small areas of simulated fur are seen in fig 55.

16   Weaving with fringes. The fringe can be either a manufactured one or made from shredded cloth. Fringes woven into cloth can make good heavy skirt edgings or occasional bands (fig 62). Bobble-fringes are also extremely effective (fig 55).

62. Weaving with fringes,
    an open fabric.

63. Free shuttling, Pamela Coates.

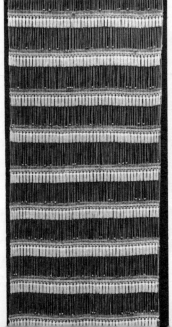

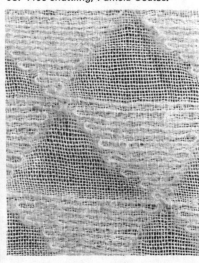

17   Weaving with braids. Braids inserted occasionally into the weft can give a rich effect and can be excellent for evening bags etc (figs 55, 62).

18   Weaving on a spaced warp with stiff wefts, like cane, metal rod, glass or perspex rods, slivers of wood, or straws, produces stiff and sometimes transparent fabrics for blinds, screens and lampshades.

19   Free shuttling. There is a basic plain weave and the free shuttling is the working on the surface with an extra yarn. This yarn is decorative only and plays no part in the construction of the cloth (fig 63).

20   Weaving with grasses and leaves, Grasses can be woven in with a fairly solid, plain weave, the heads should be left unwoven on the surface of the cloth (fig 66). Leaves can be woven in alone, with the weft meandering around them or, better still, trapped between two layers of clear acetate. This way their fragility and brittle quality is overcome. If the amount of leaf and acetate is large and yarn small the result is excellent lampshades. Make sure the size of the lamp bulb and size of shade are compatible with the use of acetate.

21   Twisting of warp ends in pairs. Doubled pairs or trebled pairs can create open fabrics, pleasant geometric patterns and also hold wefts like grasses securely in place (figs 52a, 53 and 58).

65. Plain weave with twisted weft yarns producing a 'broken' ground texture and looped texture-weaving with carpet wool and unspun fibre. Produced in a class held with the Weavers Guild of Minneapolis.

*Opposite:* Jute, raffia and polythene mats. (See page 23)

66. Weaving with grasses. Altar frontal, Irene Waller, Church of England Chapel. Royal Agricultural Show, Stoneleigh, Warwickshire.

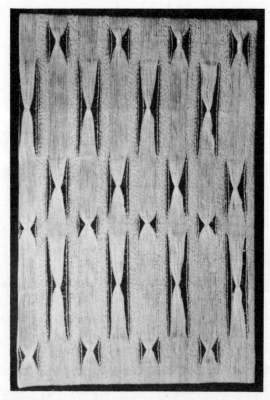

**64.** Groups of warp threads tied together, cellophane weft, Anne Istead.

22   Warp ends, in bigger bundles than are possible by twisting, can be tied together and result in pleasing geometric patterns (fig 64).

The above list gives only some of the possibilities of plain weave. There are still more. It is an excellent idea to set on a sample all-purpose warp and try out some of the ideas. Sampling on the loom in this manner invariably stimulates further ideas.

# 13 Designing

## Design Sources

Techniques and materials can be put to two purposes. They can either be used to produce the strictly practical and functional, like the mats, rugs, bags and cushions, or they can be used to bring abstract concepts into tangible being as in wallhangings and panels. The same goes for other fields of design. Clay can be used for pots or sculpture, metal for nails or abstractions and gold for a coin or a neckpiece. These two functions, practical and abstract, have not only materials and technique in common, but aesthetics, that indefinable element which gives us pleasure and satisfaction.

Now we *know* that certain things please us, flowers, trees, whatever, but on the whole we are astoundingly blind and really do not look at and see properly the world around us which is the source of everything.

It is an immensely useful practice to have a largish area of pin-boarding and shelving available on which to pin or to put interesting objects rather like a kindergarten 'nature table'. With an area like this to work with you can begin to use your eyes on things around you. Next time you go out *look* at the texture of the house wall, the drive, the pavement. You will have to stop and look closely – don't just take a passing glance; when you are on holiday particularly *look* at sand and stones and grass and tree-branches. Collect the things you can, not to make a 'collection' of anything but merely to capture those things which intrigue you visually and in a tactile sense so that you can have them around you and thus absorb them the more.

If you are fortunate enough to have a good camera, carry it around on your looking sessions and record what you see. If the results are true (in the aesthetic and not the photographically technical sense), pin your photographs up. Do likewise with magazine photos and the like and if the collection gets out of hand, acquire a folder with clear plastic envelope-like pages in which to store your reference material.

Collect also those things nearer to the practicalities of the particular matter in hand – yarns, fibre, beads, fabrics – only those which really please you, not those which bore or repel.

A marvellous way to break down any inhibitions you may have about colour is to have several large glass jars on your shelving and to drop into them fragments of anything, colourwise, which you

67. Seaweeds.

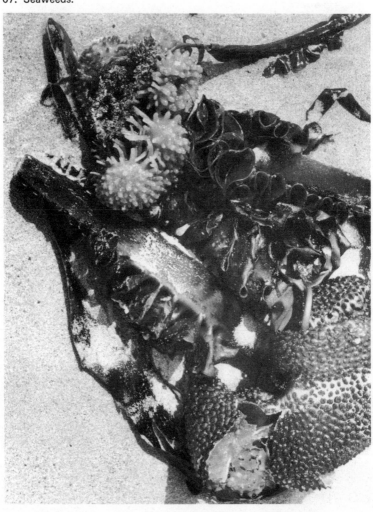

find pleasing – beads, glass, paper, yarns, fabrics. Have a jar for blues, another for greens and so on.

The net result of all this looking, observing, recording and collecting should be an increase of awareness, an increase in sensitivity and an easy and relaxed approach to using both the loom-frame and loom in a really creative and spontaneous manner. One's mind is, in fact, teeming with ideas generated by one's increased visual awareness. Consider figs 67 to 72.

68. Lobsterpots.

69. Lincoln Centre, New York.

### Assessing a Piece of Work

It is often difficult to decide whether the project on which you are engaged, *however simple*, is satisfactory or not. It is very possible to have become bogged down and to end up with something which, in spite of all the hard work, just dosen't interpret intentions correctly – and I apply this equally to the simple table mats in fig 14 as to the hangings and panels scattered through the book. But a series of practical questions and answers can help one arrive at decisions on aesthetics.

In any piece of work the total final satisfaction is made up of two elements, the craftsmanship put into it and the aesthetic content. Craftsmanship has already been dealt with exhaustively. With aesthetic content the following points can help decide whether it has been achieved and if not, why not.

First put the piece of work at some distance from you, pin it on the pinboard if it is at a stage where that is possible. If you feel bogged down, go away and have a cup of tea and then view it again. Consider the whole thing in the following sections:

70. Plant growth.

1   In general does it please me or does it not? If it does, then do no more, just carry on. If it doesn't, continue querying.
2   Colour, does it please me or not?
3   Texture, does it please me or not?
4   Graphic design, if there is one, does it please me or not?
5   Total shape, does it please me or not?
6   Shapes within the design, do they please me or not?
7   *Spaces* left by the shapes in the design, do they please me or not?
Make yourself reply 'yes' or 'no' to the questions. By breaking the whole thing down into these answerable parts you should be able to assess your own work objectively and thus produce objects which please both you and others.

**Practical Matters**

*Designing Rugs*

If you wish to design a rug, or a hanging, or an object which will end up as pure weft colour, a very good way to do it is as follows:

Draw your rug out to scale half or quarter. Rough out your design in pencil. Get as many saucers as there will be colours in the rug and into each saucer cut small snippings of individual coloured yarns, 6mm ($\frac{1}{4}$in) long, from a little bundle of yarn held in your fingers. Spread a thin layer of Copydex over the paper design. Fill in each area completely with the appropriate coloured snippings. Press down. The result will be a very fair representation of your

71. Balustrade. Port Meirion Wales.

intended rug on a small scale, and you can judge with more accuracy whether you like your design or not.

*Designing Stripes*

If, for instance, you are trying to decide on the colour and proportion of the stripes for the tapestry bag in chapter 4, do as follows:

Get a piece of cardboard say 300mm × 100mm (12in × 4in). Now wind your chosen weft yarns around this accurately and neither too tightly nor too loosely in the proposed striping. You will see a facsimile of the end product and be able to judge it accordingly.

72. Indian Palisades, Lake Huron, Canada.

## Texture-weaves

If you are designing the cushions, or something like the texture-weave in fig 55, spread Copydex thinly over a piece of stiff paper or card and glue on your proposed materials in the order and areas in which you intend them.

## Melding Colours

If you want to decide whether, for instance, a blue warp will look well with a green weft in a tabby (plain) weave, i.e. the colours will be broken up and melded together, take a strand of both colours and twist them together in the fingers. You will see the effect of the mixture.

### Isolating Designs

When producing a 'sampler' of weaves like the tapestry sampler described in chapter 7, make yourself a 'viewing card', i.e. a largish piece of card with a 100mm × 100mm (4in × 4in) hole cut in it. You can place this on the cloth and isolate certain areas of the design for individual assessment.

### Holding Designs Quickly

Sand- or glass-paper attached to your pinboard, or flat, holds yarns instantly – good for planning warps, designing stripes, or just holding small samples of yarn.

General advice about designing is – be relaxed about it. Never let the word 'design' intimidate you. Keep your eyes open to the world about you and record or collect your more interesting findings. You should soon have a mind filled with images and ideas. Instead of worrying about 'designing' it will just be a matter of finding enough hours in the day in which to give substance to your ideas.

# 14 Where Now?

The book has been devoted to introducing the absolute beginner to weaving, using simple means, inexpensive equipment and easily available materials while at the same time emphasizing good craftsmanship, sensitive design and simple concepts.

Successful accomplishment of some of the projects may already have latched you firmly on to weaving as a creative pursuit. It bears repeating to say that if you can create pleasing objects and fabrics, pleasing aesthetically and technically, with simple equipment, then you are indeed a weaver. There are enough ideas in chapter 12 alone to keep you going for a long time, still with the same, simple equipment.

However, two things may be the spur to invest in further equipment – of necessity larger and more expensive. One of these is a desire to make greater area of cloth and objects without recourse to joining. The other is to be able to use more complex cloth construction as part of the design factor. Should this be so then there is a variety of looms on the market and the suppliers' catalogues illustrate these and describe them, so acquire some catalogues (see Suppliers).

Some general advice is as follows:

If space is at a premium then table looms must be the answer. They come in considerable widths and with up to twelve or sixteen shafts (the more shafts the greater the cloth structure complexity possible). Try to arrange to have a 'trial run' on the loom before buying and make sure it has a comfortable shedding motion (lifting the shafts), not too clumsy or heavy, or it will tire you. Remember that you must have somewhere to store such a loom (under the table?) and think about the weight you will be involved in lifting before you buy.

If you have space, a floor loom with treadles is far superior to a table loom. The feet on the pedals motivate the shafts while the hands are free to weave. All very much quicker and more effective – *and* no lifting or moving involved.

When considering table and foot looms, remember that while you are buying a fairly expensive piece of equipment, you may as well buy one which will do all you may ever want to. Therefore, within limits, a wide loom with many shafts is the most useful and variable object. The shafts do not all have to be used, you use as many as you want at any given time. One factor is against the above advice: if a loom with many shafts and pedals intimidates you (though it shouldn't), or if you feel unequal to coping with something apparently complex, then go for something simple. A four-shaft 36in (915mm) foot loom is a nice, uncomplicated servant, capable of much.

An upright rug loom is a very desirable piece of equipment if rugs, tapestries and wallhangings are your objective. Gravity helps in beating down of weft and the verticality of the warp is a great aid to designing. One can stand back and view the work.

Several other pieces of equipment may be necessary in time:
A warping board, mill or posts for warping.
Roller shuttles and a quill-winder for weaving width swiftly.
A creel and a skein-winder to hold yarns.

Equipment may be bought new from the suppliers or 'used' through craft magazines or through advertizing. Never buy used equipment just because you think it is a bargain. Looms can arrive in pieces, with parts missing, and can be very difficult to put together without expert advice or a good instruction leaflet. Old looms *can* be a nasty, dusty mess, whereas new looms can be a joy to look at and to touch, not to mention to use. The converse to this, of course, is the loom which has been cared for and used skilfully and is a well run-in piece of equipment. The best general comment really, is to buy new if you can afford it, to consider the catalogues carefully before deciding and when you think you are near a decision, to have that loom demonstrated to you before purchase. The suppliers, or your local art college, if they teach weaving, or the local weavers' guild may all be willing to demonstrate a loom to you, and the time spent on consideration will be well spent; but this whole final chapter is only an 'if' chapter. Remember that some of the greatest and most creative weavers living work in the simplest possible textile terms.

# Suppliers

**Weaving Equipment**

Reeves-Dryad Ltd, Northgates, Leicester.
Harris Looms Ltd, North Grove Road, Hawkhurst, Kent.
Lillstina Looms, 6 Granville Street, Winsford, Cheshire.

**Yarns**

Reeves-Dryad Ltd, Northgates, Leicester.
Hugh Griffiths, Brookdale, Beckington, Bath.
J. Hyslop Bathgate & Co, Galashiels, Scotland.
Winwood Textile Co, Lisle Avenue, Kidderminster (rug and carpet yarns).
Atlas Handicrafts Ltd, Manchester 4.
Texere Yarns, 9 Peckover Street, Bradford.
William Hall & Co (Monsall) Ltd, 177 Stanley Road, Cheadle Hulme, Cheshire.
A. K. Graupner, Valley Road, Bradford.
T. M. Hunter, Brora, Scotland.

**Fleece**

Reeves-Dryad Ltd, Northgates, Leicester.
Hugh Griffiths, Brookdale, Beckington, Bath.

**PVA Medium**

Reeves Dryad Ltd, Northgates, Leicester, or Artists' Suppliers.

**Helpful Book Shops**

R. Drummond, 30 Hart Grove, Ealing Common, London W5. (By appointment only.)
Foyles Bookshop, 119 Charing Cross Road, London WC2.

Boddy's Bookshop, 165 Linthorpe Road, Middlesbrough, Yorkshire.
Weald Publishing Co., 48 The Pantiles, Tunbridge Wells.


## Weavers' Guilds

The Guilds of Weavers, Spinners & Dyers, 6 Queen Square, London,
WC1N 3AR. The office will give you information about the Guild
branch in your area.


## Handweaving Studios where Instruction is Available

The Handweavers Studio & Gallery, 29 Haroldstone Road, London
E17 7AN.
Colleges and Schools of Art and Evening Institutes. Specific enquiry
must be made as to whether weaving classes are held.


## Magazines

*Quarterly Journal of the Guilds of Weavers, Spinners & Dyers,*
6 Queen Square, London WC1N 3AR.
*Crafts Magazine*, 28 Haymarket, London SW1Y 4YZ.
*Shuttle Spindle & Dyepot*, Journal of the Handweavers Guild of
America, 1013 Farmington Avenue, W. Hartford, Connecticut,
USA.
*Craft Horizons*, Journal of the American Crafts Council, 44 W. 53rd
Street, New York, USA.

# Bibliography

Albers, Anni, *On Weaving*, Studio Vista, London, 1966; Wesleyan University Press, Middleton, Connecticut, USA, 1963.

Atwater, Mary, *The Shuttle Craft Book of American Handweaving*, Macmillan, New York, 1951.

Atwater, Mary, *Byways in Handweaving*, Macmillan, New York, 1954.

Beutlich, Tadek, *The Technique of Woven Tapestry*, Batsford, London, 1967; Watson Guptill, New York, 1967.

Birrell, Verla, *The Textile Arts*, Harper, New York, 1959.

Black, Mary, *New Key to Weaving*, Bruce Publishing Co, Milwaukee, 1957.

Blumenau. L., *The Art and Craft of Handweaving*, 1955.

Blumenau. L., *Creative Design in Wallhangings*, 1967.

Chetwynd, Hilary, *Simple Weaving,* Studio Vista, London 1975; Watson Guptill, New York, 1969.

Collingwood, Peter, *The Techniques of Rug Weaving*, Faber & Faber, London 1968; Watson Guptill, New York, 1967.

Constantine, Mildred and Larsen, Jack, *Beyond Craft, the Art Fabric*, Van Nostrand, New York, 1973.

Cyrus, U., *Manual of Swedish Handweaving*, 1956.

Grierson, Ronald, *Woven Rugs*, Dryad, Leicester, UK.

Halsey, Mike and Youngmark, Lore, *Foundations of Weaving*, David & Charles, Newton Abbot, 1974.

Hooper, Luther, *Handloom Weaving*, Pitman, New York, 1920.

Kauffman, Ruth, *The New American Tapestry*, Reinhold, New York, 1968.

Kirby, Mary, *Designing on the Loom*, Studio Publications, London and New York, 1955. Reprinted 1974, Select Books, California.

Kuenzi, André, *La Nouvelle Tapisserie*, Bonvent, Paris, 1973.

Rainey, Sarita, *Weaving without a Loom*, Davis Publications, Worcester, Mass., USA, 1966.

Rainey, Sarita, *Wallhangings, Designing with Fabric and Thread*, Davis Publications, Worcester, Mass., USA, 1966.

Regensteiner, Elsa, *The Art of Weaving*, 1970.

Seagroatt, Margaret, *Rug Weaving for Beginners*, Studio Vista, London, 1971.

Simpson & Weir, *The Weavers Craft*, Dryad, Leicester, UK.

Tattersall, C., *Carpet Knotting and Weaving*, V. & A. Museum, London, 1920.

Tidball, H., *Build or Buy a Loom,* Shuttlecraft Guild, Craft and Hobby Book Service, Pacific Grove, California.

Tovey, John, *The Technique of Weaving*, Batsford, London; Reinhold, New York, 1965.

Tovey, John, *Weaves and Pattern Drafting*, Batsford, London; Reinhold, New York, 1969.

Thorpe, Azalea and Larsen, Jack, *Elements of Weaving*, Doubleday, New York, 1967.

Waller, Irene, *Thread, an Art Form*, Studio Vista, London, 1973.

Wilson, Jean, *Weaving is for Anyone*, Reinhold, New York; Studio Vista, London, 1967.

Znamierowski, Nell *Step by Step Weaving*, Golden Press, New York, 1967.

*Tablet Weaving*, Dryad, Leicester, UK.

# Glossary

ARC  The weft yarn put into the warp in a curve to obviate warp pulling-in or 'waisting'.

BASKET-WEAVE  Plain or 'tabby' weave with doubled wefts.

BEAMING  Winding the warp on to the back or warp roller of a loom.

BUTTERFLY  A small hank of yarn made on the fingers of the left hand, to be used as a means of inserting weft when no shuttle is available.

CARDING  The combing and straightening of wool fibres, by implements called carders as a preliminary process to spinning.

CROSS (In the warp)  The point at which, in a long warp destined for a roller loom, the individual warp ends pass alternately over and under or under and over a pair of sticks passing through them at right angles. The purpose of the cross is to keep each individual warp end in its own place.

CROSS-STICKS  The sticks wider than the warp and with holes at either end, which pass across and through the warp to secure the crossed threads.

FELL (of the cloth)  The weaving edge.

FOOT LOOM  A floor loom equipped with treadles for the operating of the shafts on which the individual heddles are mounted.

FOUR-SHAFT LOOM  A loom, either on a table or standing on the floor, equipped with four shafts on which the string or metal individual heddles are mounted. Looms can have up to sixteen or more shafts.

GAUZE WEAVE  A weave in which the warp threads cross over one another in pairs, or some other sequence. The result is that a light sparse weft can be held firmly and thus light-weight fabrics produced.

HEDDLE  The individual metal or string eye or loop through which each warp end is passed in order to manipulate it.

HEDDLE-HOOK    A fine hook for threading the warp ends through the heddles.

HEMSTITCH    An embroidery or needlework stitch used to secure fringed edges.

HOPSACK    Plain or tabby weave with double warp and weft.

LOOM    A frame of some sort on which to stretch a warp, with some mechanism, however simple or complex, for parting the warp threads in order to insert the weft, and for beating down.

PICK    One row or insertion of weft.

PILE    Lengths of yarn cut or looped, long or short, fine or coarse, springing from the surface of the cloth.

PLAIN WEAVE    (Also known as tabby weave.) The simplest weave there is, one pick passing over and under the warp ends, the next under and over.

QUILL    The small bobbin of weft yarn which is inserted into a roller shuttle.

QUILL-WINDER    Mechanism for winding quills.

REED    A piece of equipment made of metal which serves to keep the warp threads spaced at the correct distance apart.

REED HOOK    A flat hook for threading the warp ends through the reed.

RIGID HEDDLE    A row of metal heddles held together in a rigid frame. Gives a plain or tabby weave only.

RIGID HEDDLE LOOM    The table loom which employs the rigid heddle.

ROLLER SHUTTLE    Shuttles shaped like boats which take a quill of yarn in the centre. These roll through the shed and are necessary for wide cloth.

SAMPLER    A piece of cloth which is a series of experiments and explorations.

SELVEDGE    The warp ends at the two side edges of the cloth, generally spaced more closely than the body of the warp in order to produce a firm weave.

SHED    The opening between the warp ends through which the weft passes.

SHED-STICK    The stick which is passed through the warp on a frame-loom to give one of the two sheds.

SHUTTLE    The mechanism on which the weft yarn is wound to facilitate its progress through the warp.

SHUTTLE-STICK    The simplest form of shuttle. A flat stick, concave at each end.

SPINNING    The process of drawing out fibre and giving it twist to create yarn.

TABBY WEAVING    See plain weaving.

TABLE LOOM    Any loom which rests on a table rather than the floor.

TAPESTRY    Plain weave in which the weft is beaten down hard to cover the warp entirely.

TEASING    The process of pulling out wool fibres to release dirt and rubbish.

TURKISH KNOT    A pile knot passing around two warp threads.

WAISTING    Pulling the cloth in widthwise when weaving.

WARP    The longitudinal threads placed upon the loom.

WARP END    One individual warp thread.

WARP STICK    Extra sticks, provided with a roller loom, with which to beam the warp to keep it regular and smooth.

WARPING BOARD    Warping posts set permanently into a board.

WARPING MILL    Posts set on to an upright frame which turns round, thus the warp is made in a spiral, and the warper stands still.

WARPING POSTS    Separate and movable posts on which to make a warp.

WEAVING NEEDLE    A long bodkin with large eye and blunt tip.

WEFT    The yarn which traverses the warp from side to side.

# Index

Compiled by *Susan Kennedy*

Entries in *italics* refer to whole chapters or subsections